Foundations of IT Service Management

The *Unofficial* ITIL® v3 Foundations Course in a Book

Brady Orand

PUBLISHED BY

ITILYaBrady

www.ITILYaBrady.com

Copyright © 2009 by Brady Orand

ISBN 1-4392-2633-4

Preface

Writing a book is a huge endeavor. It was much more than I originally anticipated. I started this book in 2006, applying what I learned about ITIL® and what I continued to learn from each ITIL® Foundations class that I taught. By the time I came close to finishing the first draft, ITIL® version 3 was on the horizon so I waited to see what was new about ITIL® v3.

ITIL® v3 added so much new information that I had to take the time necessary to completely understand how this new material could be incorporated into what I had already accomplished. Of course, with the combination of the new material and having taught dozens more classes and hundreds of students thus learning more about the subtleties of ITIL® v3 and how students learn, an almost complete re-write was in order.

Part of the delay in getting a book to print is trying to make it absolutely perfect. Every time I read a section, I think that I could re-word a sentence to make it just a bit more clear or add a section to elaborate on a point. Also, with every class I teach, I learn more and more about IT Service Management. This learning usually occurs when I see the light bulb go on in a student's eyes and I know that I said something that helped them to grasp the material better. That light bulb effect provides me with more insight into what needs to be added to the book to make it better understood.

With all of these new ideas on how to present the material, it is a never ending battle of what to put into the book and what to change. I finally had to make the decision to stop adding and get it to the printer. After all, a book does no good if no one has access to it.

I wrote this book with you, the reader, in mind. After many years in the IT industry, I found ITIL® to be my "calling," so to speak. I thoroughly enjoy teaching ITIL® classes and get a feeling of satisfaction when students start talking about how they can take some of these newly learned concepts and apply them in their organization.

You are reading this book for a reason. I have found that most students learn about ITIL® and take the ITIL® Foundation exam primarily because they want to apply these concepts in their organization. Other students attend the classes because their employer insisted that they go. And there are others who simply want to learn more about something that they heard is in hot demand in the industry. Whatever your reason, I hope this book meets your needs.

This book is my small way to change the world - one student at a time. I have strived to make the material as understandable as possible for the broadest audience possible. However, if there is anything that you may not understand or need clarification on, please feel free to ask. Also if there are suggestions that you want to offer, I'm always open to hear them.

Brady Orand
Brady@ITILYaBrady.com
January 1, 2009

About This Book

This book was written to prepare you for your ITIL® v3 Foundation exam. Through the chapters of this book, you will be introduced to the Service Lifecycle and the processes described within each of the Service Lifecycle stages. More importantly, you will learn how these processes work together to provide IT Services.

In addition to this book, there are many resources available online to assist you with your exam preparation. Some of the resources you may find valuable can be found on my website at www.ITILYaBrady.com. At the time of this writing, there are study guides, audio reviews, sample exam questions and study material checklists.

Chapters in this book are organized around the major topics present in the finalized syllabus provided by APM Group, the organization responsible for the ITIL® certification syllabi. This fourth version of the syllabus is expected to go into effect with examinations around May, 2009.

Even though this book is designed around the syllabus published by APMG, my desire through this course is not only to prepare you for the ITIL® Foundations certification exam, but also to provide insight into how ITIL® may improve your IT organization. While many courses and books exist to convey material to you simply to help you pass the exam, I want to ensure that you improve and change the way you look at IT.

However, I also understand that the primary desire of the reader is probably to pass the ITIL® Foundations exam. While almost everything in this course is candidate for exam questions, there are certain key things that are far more likely to be on the exam. These items are focused on in the Chapter Review sections at the end of each chapter.

ABOUT THE AUTHOR

I have been an ITIL® instructor since 2005. Even though I had worked in the IT field for close to two decades, I did not truly understand IT until my first exposure to ITIL® three years earlier through my ITIL® Foundations course. Ever since then, I have been pursuing my ITIL® education to be the best instructor that I can possibly be. Along this path, I have obtained many of the ITIL® v2 certifications, including the Service Manager certification.

When ITIL v3 was published, I started reading the books and haven't stopped. A couple of the ITIL® v3 books I've read four or five times - always finding something new! As a result of all of this learning, I have accomplished the feat of successfully passing all of the ITIL® v3 exams, including all ten of the intermediate and advanced exams available to date.

I started my career as an intern at a small microchip company you may have heard of, called Intel®. My job there was to develop parts of a software product for Novell® networks. Even though this was the early 1990's, I still run across some people who continue use the products that I helped create.

I then went on to a company that focuses solely on software, BMC Software®, where I was responsible for a line of integration products that integrated BMC's products with other vendor products. This is where I really started learning the complexities of managing the IT infrastructure. This is also where I started my consulting and training career.

After BMC, my career led to a big-five consulting firm where I learned what "big projects" really are. As part of a 1,000-person project, I had the opportunity to learn more about the operational aspects of IT and how critical effective processes are to the success of such a large organization. I often look back on this experience and think about how we did things that were right, how we did things that were wrong and how both of these are addressed by ITIL®.

My first true teaching opportunity came when I then joined a smaller consulting company based outside of Chicago. As the ITIL Practice Manager, my job was to create offerings around the concepts of IT Service Management. The majority of my time was spent building training offerings and delivering this training. This is where I found that I truly enjoyed delivering training. However, the travel wasn't as much fun as it used to be.

I now work independently as a trainer, training course provider and consultant. I deliver training on behalf several companies, but the travel is much more tolerable. This also gives me the opportunity to pursue many of my own interests, such as study guides, exam preparation material, white papers, and other pursuits.

In my courses, I combine the book learning with practical experience from the many varied roles that I have had in my career. In this book, I have attempted to reflect this style on paper.

Contents

Introduction to ITIL®

Processes, Functions and Roles

Service Strategy Overview

SERVICE DESIGN OVERVIEW

SERVICE TRANSITION OVERVIEW

SERVICE OPERATION OVERVIEW

CONTINUAL SERVICE IMPROVEMENT OVERVIEW

SERVICE STRATEGY SHARED ACTIVITIES

SERVICE STRATEGY PROCESSES

SERVICE DESIGN PROCESSES

6

SERVICE TRANSITION PROCESSES

SERVICE OPERATION PROCESSES

CONTINUAL SERVICE IMPROVEMENT PROCESSES

SERVICE OPERATION FUNCTIONS

TOOL AND TECHNOLOGY CONSIDERATIONS

List of Figures

1

Getting Started

Introduction

This book introduces you to the concepts of IT Service Management based on ITIL®. In my many years of providing ITIL® training, the one thing that remains constant is that every individual has a different learning style. Some people prefer reading while others prefer live or video presentations. In all cases, however, I have found that almost everyone responds well to analogies.

In this book, the restaurant business is used as the analogy through the introduction of a fictitious entrepreneur, Geppetto Garcia, and his company. Geppetto's restaurant business can teach us a lot about the concepts of service. After all, restaurants with poor service don't last long. After exploring Geppetto's startup problems and what he learned from them, we will explore how Geppetto Garcia's integrated the concepts of service into their corporation's IT department.

Through this exploration, the concepts of IT Service Management are explored and applied to Geppetto Garcia's through a case study. I hope you find this exploration useful and it assists with your retention of the information in the following pages.

Geppetto Garcia's

Geppetto Garcia, a multi-cultural American born son of second generation immigrants, grew up working in his cousin's restaurant for years. Geppetto's desire to cook was immense. His dream was always to have a restaurant of his own. He longed for a restaurant that would cater to every customer's desires, and to serve meals that would please any appetite.

At the age of 28, and after investing all of his life savings, Geppetto opened his first restaurant, named Geppetto Garcia's. Geppetto's 25 table restaurant opened in a prime location to serve both the lunch time business crowd, as well as the before and after theater diners. Geppetto's restaurant employed a kitchen staff of three full-time employees, four wait staff, and four part-time helpers to bus tables and wash dishes.

Opening day was slow. Geppetto wanted to see how the walk in traffic was before he started advertising. His first customer, a lone businessman at lunch walked in between meetings. Geppetto met the gentleman at the door and promptly seated him.

"What can I get you?" asked Geppetto.

"What do you have?" asked the businessman.

"Whatever your heart desires, I'll make it for you!" was Geppetto's response.

"Hmmm," says the businessman. "I've been thinking about my Czech grandmother's goulash lately. She used to make it for me when I was a kid."

"You got it!" replied Geppetto.

Geppetto promptly entered the kitchen to make his first customer the finest Czech goulash he could. However, Geppetto had never made goulash before and he had to look it up in his recipe book. Unfortunately, he did not have a recipe book that had goulash in it. Turning to the Internet, he quickly looked up "Czech Goulash" and found the following recipe.

Czech Goulash[1]

¼ cup shortening

2 cloves garlic, minced

1 ½ pounds cubed beef

1 medium onion, chopped

¼ teaspoon sweet paprika

½ teaspoon caraway seeds

Salt and pepper to taste

---

1   Source: Recipe Gold Mine at www.recipegoldmine.com

2 cups water

2 tablespoons flour

In a cast iron Dutch oven, sauté onion in shortening. Add garlic and sauté until translucent. Add meat, onion, paprika, caraway seeds, salt and pepper. Brown well.

Add ½ cup of the water and simmer, covered, until meat is tender, about 1 hour.

Sprinkle flour over drippings in the pan and stir until brown. Add remaining water. Simmer 10 to 20 minutes.

Serve over cooked egg noodles.

Serves 6-8.

Geppetto was excited. He had all of these ingredients except the sweet paprika. All he had was regular paprika but the recipe called for sweet paprika. Geppetto left the recipe for his kitchen staff to start and went to the gourmet grocer to procure some sweet paprika.

30 minutes later when Geppetto returned, the goulash was ready for the paprika. Once the ¼ teaspoon of sweet paprika was added, Geppetto went to the dining room to check on his customer.

Noticing that the businessman was drumming his fingers impatiently, Geppetto approached the gentleman.

"Your goulash is being prepared," said Geppetto.

"Sounds great, but I have a meeting in 30 minutes so I must leave very soon," said the gentleman.

"I'll see what I can do to speed it up!" responded Geppetto.

Geppetto then returned to the kitchen.

"Cook faster!" he yelled at the kitchen staff.

Geppetto then turned up the heat (both literally and figuratively) to get the goulash to cook faster.

Just over an hour later, the goulash was ready. Geppetto spooned the goulash on a plate with some egg noodles, garnished it with parsley and headed to the dining room. Upon entering the dining room, Geppetto walked in only to find an empty table where the businessman had been.

For the next week, Geppetto experienced similar situations over and over again. In his quest to provide whatever meal the customer requests, he could only very rarely prepare the dish the customer asked for before they became frustrated and left. Geppetto was left with fully cooked Chateaubriand, Buffalo burgers, grilled duck and lamb chops. While he and his kitchen staff were preparing fantastic dishes, there was no way they could cook just anything to order.

The first week was miserable for Geppetto. After the first week, the kitchen staff was threatening to quit because of trying to please everyone by making so many different dishes. The wait staff was looking for other positions because customers were not leaving tips. But who would? To make things worse, the food that Geppetto was purchasing was going bad because he would buy in bulk to save money only to use a small part of it while the rest went unused. Geppetto was spending a lot of money to pay salaries, rent and debts, not to mention the costs for the food suppliers. He was running his business at a significant loss.

Geppetto quickly realized that he could not be everything to everyone. First, he needed to determine his menu. Ideally, his menu would consist of meals that would minimize the variety of supplies that he would require to those that would be used – thus limiting food that would rot before it was used.

His meal selection would also have to be within the limits of his kitchen staff. The meals should be able to be prepared through a series of well-defined steps thus simplifying the preparation. This would also result in the meals being predictable and consistent.

Geppetto also realized that he had a lot of talent and creativity in the kitchen staff. He decided that he would involve his kitchen staff in these decisions and take advantage of their capabilities. His kitchen staff also represented diverse backgrounds, Mediterranean, Asian and South American. Together they decided to select recipes from different continents and countries and provide a menu representing meals from around the world.

Therefore Geppetto developed the following criteria for meals that he would serve:

- Meals would be prepared from fresh ingredients
- Meals would be prepared from ingredients that could be used in other meals or ingredients with a longer shelf life (such as dried spices, frozen foods and dried staples)
- Meals would represent specialties from each culture and country

- Meals would be repeatable, consistent and prepared as much as possible prior to the lunch and dinner rush
- Meals would be moderately priced for customers providing a balance between quality, cost, speed and ambiance

Geppetto scoured his recipe books and the Internet for recipes that met these criteria. From the thousands of recipes that Geppetto found, he and his team found many that met these criteria or could be modified to meet these criteria. Geppetto and his team selected 44 recipes that met the criteria and also met the needs of his target customers. These recipes provided everything they needed to prepare entrees and desserts. Geppetto also had his grandmother's Pasta Primavera recipe that he added to the list, making the total number of items that would go on his menu 45.

Geppetto then enlisted the wait staff to help design the menu. When designing the menu, they included a section for entrees and desserts. They quickly realized that appetizers, soups, and salads were missing. Using the ingredients included in the previously selected recipes, Geppetto and his teams developed appetizers, soups and salads that could be quickly prepared and added these to the menu.

Based on this menu, Geppetto worked with his kitchen staff to be able to prepare these meals by creating processes that could be reused or modified for the specific menu. While his kitchen staff had some issues at first, they quickly learned to create these meals on demand by establishing specific processes and procedures to prepare the meals. Helping to achieve these efficiencies and improved delivery of meals was preparing parts of the meals beforehand. The more the team could get done prior to the lunch and dinner rush, the better prepared they were when the restaurant became busy.

Geppetto also worked with his wait staff to develop processes and procedures in handling customers, including timely seating, taking orders, and handling special requests. Just as his kitchen staff realized, the more they could get done prior to the busy times, the easier it was to provide great service.

Within a very short period, Geppetto Garcia's became very popular with his target market of business professionals at lunch and the theater crowd in the evenings. Once the word got out, Geppetto Garcia's became popular with the weekend brunch and late lunch diners as well.

Over time, Geppetto Garcia owned one of the most popular restaurants in the region and began to expand to other cities. Geppetto realized that the business was bigger than he thought and began opening specialty restaurants that focused on expanded menus of specific regional cuisines. These restaurants include Garcia's Cantina serving Mexican fare,

GC's Steak House with a mid-range menu around steaks and chops, GC's Smokehouse focusing on southern-style barbecue, Geppetto's Italian featuring entrees from the various regions of Italy and Geppetto's Sports Bar with a full bar and a pub-style menu. A new endeavor for Geppetto Garcia's is the GC's American Grill, a high-end dining experience that caters to the most discriminating diner. This restaurant even features the Czech Goulash recipe – the first meal that he prepared for a customer!

Geppetto Garcia's grew so big that a corporate office was established and within 6 years, the company went public, offering stock that was traded on the NASDAQ with the stock symbol GPTO. This enabled Geppetto to open 212 restaurants throughout the United States with plans to expand to areas outside the United States.

Geppetto learned a lot from his experience running a restaurant. He learned that it is impossible to be able to provide anything that someone could ask for but instead to focus on things that customers need. This permits focus on specific activities that can be standardized to create consistency. He also realized that communication with customers is critical. This communication is performed in many ways – by greeting them upon arrival, menus, asking how their meal is, ensuring they are satisfied when they leave, and also through email and web surveys to ensure that their needs are being met.

Geppetto's new corporation needed to keep these lessons in mind. Even though running a company is very different than running a single restaurant, most of the basics remain the same. Therefore, Geppetto will ensure that all aspects of the corporation will adopt these basic principles and look for ways to improve services to customers and ensure that these services balance cost and quality with the customer's needs.

The Growth of Geppetto Garcia's

Geppetto is a restaurateur at heart. Restaurants are what he knows best. As the business grew and the corporation evolved, Geppetto hired people with specialized skills and knowledge to handle specific areas of the business. One of these areas was Information Technology (IT). Geppetto could barely send an email, but it doesn't stop him from running a successful business. To fill the need for an IT leader, Geppetto found Mark Renner, a man who understands both IT and customer service.

Mark Renner, the new Chief Information Officer, recognized the need for IT to be focused on satisfying the customers of IT. Just like when Geppetto researched for recipes, Mark searched for best practices in providing IT services. Mark discovered the IT Infrastructure Library.

Restaurants and IT

If the above fictional accounting of Geppetto and his restaurant seems outrageous, it is. No restaurant that I know of would dream of opening its doors without having some form of menu or offering to their customers. Restaurants cannot attempt to provide any requested meal on demand like that. It is impossible to create every possible meal on demand and be able to meet the customer's needs.

Restaurants are often low-margin businesses due to intense competition. They make very little profit from an individual meal. They must therefore make their profit through larger volume business in order to survive. To provide higher volume, restaurants must be as effective and efficient as possible. This is done by attracting customers to their offerings, as well as developing and establishing processes that are definable, repeatable, and consistent.

If restaurants realize this, then why doesn't IT? Many of the IT organizations that I have visited attempt to be everything to everyone. They operate without a menu, have very little defined processes and only communicate with their customers when they have to through ill-defined channels. This is made even more difficult since many of them can't identify who their customers are!

IT can learn a lot from Geppetto and his experience with building a corporation from a single restaurant. In this book, we are going to explore the IT Infrastructure Library and how Geppetto would approach many of these concepts based on his common sense approach. This exploration will assist you, the reader, in preparing for your ITIL® version 3 Foundation exam, formally known as the Foundation Certificate in IT Service Management.

Geppetto Garcia's New Services

Emil Delgassi, Geppetto Garcia's Chief Operating Officer, recognized that restaurant customers want to share their enjoyment of the various Geppetto Garcia restaurants with their friends and family. One of the ways in which they want to do this is through using gift cards. Gift cards have become very popular over the years and are now sold not only at the business that the gift card is for, but also at other retail stores including grocery stores, department stores and drug stores.

Emil's idea involves the creation of gift cards that are customized for each of the restaurant brands that they have. However, not all restaurant brands will choose to have gift cards so it must first be determined which restaurants will participate in the gift card idea.

Another idea that Emil has seen work with other restaurants is "car-side" service. Car-side service targets those customers who desire a meal from one of the many restaurants in the Geppetto Garcia family but who do not have time to dine within the restaurant. This take out service involves a customer calling the restaurant or ordering on their web site and then coming to pick up their meal at the time indicated when the order has been placed.

During our exploration of ITIL®, We will see how these new services take advantage of the concepts within ITIL to ensure that they are targeted toward the right customers, designed well, transitioned into operation with a minimum of risk and can be operated as efficiently and effectively as possible.

OBJECTIVES OF THIS BOOK

This book will help you in preparing for the ITIL® v3 Foundations exam. In addition, you should complete this book with a better understanding of ITIL®, the Service Lifecycle, and the processes within each of the Service Lifecycle stages.

To help you study for the ITIL® v3 Foundations exam, there is certain information in this course that you should know. ITIL® describes the Service Lifecycle. The Service Lifecycle has five distinct stages; Service Strategy, Service Design, Service Transition, Service Operation and Continual Service Improvement. Each of these stages has the following:

Inputs and outputs

Describes the relationship between this stage and others

Principles and key concepts

Describes the purpose and approach to the stage of the Service Lifecycle

Processes and Functions

Describes the processes that are inherent within each stage of the Service Lifecycle

Functions are described in the Service Operation stage of the Service Lifecycle

In addition, each process within the Service Lifecycle stage has its own goals and objectives, key concepts, activities, Key Performance Indicators (KPI's), Critical Success Factors (CSF's), and challenges. As you will see, some processes are focused on more than others by discussing all of these topics. Other processes are not presented in as much detail, but still convey the objectives and key concepts for the process. At a minimum, you should know the purpose of the process, key concepts and how the process interacts with other processes, while certain processes require additional knowledge for the exam.

CERTIFICATION REQUIREMENTS

The ITIL® Foundations Certification exam is required in order to obtain the Foundations in Service Management certificate. This certification is the first in a progressively advancing series of certifications available in IT Service Management.

In order to obtain the Foundations level certification, you must successfully pass the Foundations certification exam. This exam is a 1 hour, 40 question, multiple choice exam where guesses are not penalized. In other words, don't leave any answers blank.

In order to pass the exam, you must get 26 or more questions correct. This represents a 65% grade on the exam. Exam results are not publicized only an overall pass or fail result. A 65% is just as good as a 95% - both lead to the certification.

There are several routes you can pursue to take the exam. The examination providers that I recommend are Thompson Prometric and Pearson VUE. Both of these providers specialize in conducting on-demand certification exams. I have taken Microsoft certification exams from them, as well as Project Management (PMI®) certification exams and the process to take an exam is fairly straightforward.

You can contact Thompson Prometric at www.prometric.com and Pearson VUE at www.vue.com for more information on taking the ITIL® exam.

Specific information for registering for the ITIL® Foundations exam is available on the www.ITILYaBrady.com website.

QUALIFICATION SCHEME

Upon completion of the ITIL® Foundations certification exam, you are eligible to continue your IT Service Management education to pursue other certifications. The ITIL® v3 Foundations certification is a prerequisite for these intermediate courses.

There are two paths through the education opportunities, the IT Service Lifecycle Stream and the IT Service Capability Modules. The Service Lifecycle Stream addresses each of the Service Lifecycle stages in five courses. The Capabilities Stream addresses specific concepts within the Service Lifecycle regardless of the stage of the Service Lifecycle involved. These courses show that many of the activities and processes have involvement in more than one discrete Service Lifecycle stage.

Once the required number of courses is completed successfully in a given path, you have the opportunity to take the Managing through the Lifecycle course. Successful completion of this course, along with the prerequisite credits will earn you the ITIL® Expert Certification.

After the ITIL® Expert, it is possible to pursue an Advanced Service Management Professional Diploma. At the time of this writing, details on this diploma are still being developed.

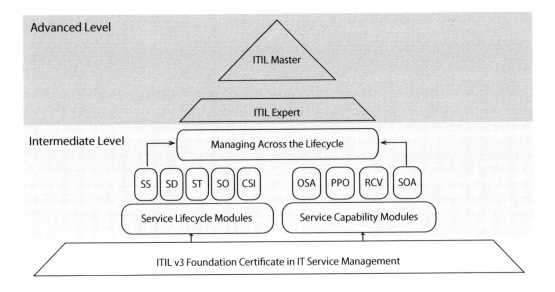

Figure 1 - ITIL Qualification Scheme

The intermediate courses follow two streams – the Service Lifecycle stream and Service Capability stream. These two streams are summarized below:

ITIL® Service Lifecycle Stream Courses

Service Strategy

The Service Strategy course provides an in-depth understanding of the Service Strategy stage of the Service Lifecycle. In the Service Strategy course, students gain an understanding of the principles of service strategy, defining services and market spaces, conducting strategic assessments as well as the processes of Financial Management, Demand Management and Service Portfolio Management.

- Benefits of establishing a strategic view to services within IT
- Principles of developing market spaces, defining services and designing a service portfolio
- Determining and managing demand for services
- Conducting strategic assessments
- The specific Service Strategy processes of
    - Service Portfolio Management
    - Financial Management
    - Demand Management

Service Design

The Service Design course provides an in-depth understanding of the Service Design stage of the Service Lifecycle. In the Service Design course, students gain an understanding of the principles of service design, Service Design activities, concepts, inputs and outputs.

- Benefits of proper design of services and changes to services
- Greater understanding of the activities involved in designing services in accordance with best practice
- Considerations for all aspects of services that must be designed
- The specific processes in Service Design of

- Service Level Management
- Service Catalog Management
- Capacity Management
- Availability Management
- IT Service Continuity Management
- Information Security Management
- Supplier Management

Service Transition

The Service Transition course provides an in-depth understanding of the Service Transition stage of the Service Lifecycle. In the Service Transition course, students gain an understanding of the principles of service transition, management and control of Service Transition activities, and Service Transition activities around communications, commitment and organizational change.

- Benefits of transitioning of services into production environments
- Establishing control of components that make up services
- Managing and communicating organizational change
- Specific Service Transition processes of
    - Transition Planning and Support
    - Service Asset and Configuration Management
    - Evaluation
    - Service Validation and Testing
    - Change Management
    - Release and Deployment Management
    - Knowledge Management

Service Operation

The Service Operation course provides an in-depth understanding of the Service Operation stage of the Service Lifecycle. In this course, students gain an understanding of the principles of Service Operation, its activities, concepts, inputs and outputs, and the functions included.

- Principles of effective and efficient Service Operation in accordance with best practices
- Organizing Service Operation
- Roles and Responsibilities of the functions within Service Operation and how they contribute to all stages of the Service Lifecycle
- The processes within Service Operation of
    - Event Management
    - Incident Management
    - Request Fulfillment
    - Problem Management
    - Access Management

Continual Service Improvement

The Continual Service Improvement course provides an in-depth understanding of the Continual Service Improvement stage of the Service Lifecycle. In the Continual Service Improvement course, students gain an understanding of the principles, methods and techniques of Continual Service Improvement.

- How Continual Service Improvement integrates within all Service Lifecycle stages
- Measurement and reporting of services
- Continual Service Improvement and Service Level Management
- The importance of properly defining metrics and measurements to support the organizational mission
- Return on Investment concepts
- Various business questions for Continual Service Improvement
- The 7-Step Improvement process

ITIL® Service Capability Stream

Service Offerings and Agreement (SO&A)

The Service Offerings and Agreements course provides the student with a deep understanding of the concepts associated with IT as a Service Provider. Within this course, the student will obtain knowledge relating to establishing and maintaining relationships between IT as a Service Provider and the business as a Customer of the Service Provider. Starting with development of a Service Portfolio, the student will understand the structure of the documented services and agreements that document the roles and responsibilities of those who deliver and support services to the customer.

- Documenting services and requirements within the Service Portfolio
- Production and management of the Service Catalog
- The set of agreements that document the roles and responsibilities of the various parties involved in providing services
- Production and maintenance of Service Level Agreements
- Using Demand Management to identify patterns of business activity
- Specific processes including
    - Service Portfolio Management
    - Service Catalog Management
    - Service Level Management
    - Demand Management
    - Supplier Management
    - Financial Management

Operational Support and Analysis (OS&A)

The Operational Support and Analysis intermediate course teaches the student the key principles involved in effective operational support of services within the domain of the IT Service Provider. This course also teaches the roles and responsibilities required to provide efficient and effective operational support of services.

- Understanding of the processes and process activities involved in providing operational support and analysis of services

- Effective structures for organizing roles for operational support and analysis of services
- Operational activities of processes contained within non-operational Service Lifecycle stages
- Key processes within Operational Support and Analysis
    - Event management
    - Request Fulfillment
    - Incident Management
    - Problem Management
    - Access Management

Planning, Protection and Optimization (PP&O)

The Planning, Protection and Optimization course immerses the student into the activities involved in planning services and changes to services, protecting services and the business from outages and disasters, as well as ensuring the right levels of service availability, capacity, security and continuity are provided in a cost-effective manner. Through this course, students will learn the concepts and activities involved in planning and ensuring the quality of services and changes to those services.

- Elements involved with the practice of planning, protection and optimization of services
- Ensuring the capabilities to realize successful designs of services through managing capacity, availability, IT service continuity and information security
- Understanding the elements involved to support the overall Business Continuity Management efforts of the organization
- Understanding how information security plays a part in the overall corporate governance framework
- The roles and responsibilities involved in planning, protection and optimization of services and changes to services
- Specific processes involved in the planning, protection and optimization of services including
    - Capacity Management

- Availability Management
- IT Service Continuity Management
- Information Security Management
- Demand Management

Release, Control and Validation (RCV)

The Release, Control and Validation course teaches students the concepts and activities present in the processes involved in the successful release, control and validation of services and changes to services before entering the production environment. This course is recommended for those who want to ensure successful transition of changes to service and organizational change within their environment.

- Processes across the Service Lifecycle pertaining to the capability of Release, Control and Validation of services and changes to services
- Ensuring successful service transition through managing and controlling change
- Assuring the integrity and quality of a service transition through proper service validation and testing
- Minimizing risk through periodic evaluation of transition activities and processes
- Assuring committed service level performance through fulfilling requests
- Roles and responsibilities involved in effective release, control and evaluation of transition activities
- Specific processes involved in Release, Control and Validation including
    - Change Management
    - Service Release and Deployment Management
    - Service Validation and Testing
    - Service Asset and Configuration Management
    - Knowledge Management
    - Request Fulfillment
    - Service Evaluation

2

SERVICE MANAGEMENT AS A PRACTICE

OVERVIEW

Managing IT today involves far more than just managing the technology within IT. Businesses are demanding more from IT services. IT Service Management is a different perspective on managing IT. Instead of managing IT technology, IT Service Management involves organizing IT as a set of services that are aligned to the business needs.

By changing the way we view IT, from a technology provider to a service provider, we focus on the outcomes that are important to the business while simultaneously changing the culture within IT to become more professional and better aligned to the needs of the business.

ISSUES FACING IT

As IT has evolved over the years, it has become more than the enabling organization that it started to be. Today's IT organization is a critical component to just about every aspect of business. Technology has embedded itself into every aspect of business that IT must evolve to support these advances. Unfortunately, IT as an organization suffers because managing technology the way it was done in the past is no longer sufficient. The stakes are far too high for the business to tolerate mistakes.

As technology has advanced and business use of technology has grown, IT has struggled with meeting the new demands. In my experience, IT organizations struggle with keeping the current environment operating to meet existing business needs resulting in a purely reactive environment. This leaves little time or energy for the constant new requirements that arrive on a daily basis.

As a result, IT is constantly suffering from lack of appreciation for their hard work and efforts. The business fails to see the value that IT provides, and IT has a difficult time communicating this value. At the end of the year, the costs of IT are a focus that leads to budget cuts and head count reduction while, at the same time, the requirement to provide better service increases.

The key issues for IT are that they are not able to improve because of lack of time, proper measurements and, frankly, lack of motivation. Projects that are conducted for the business are constantly being interrupted because of operational issues. When the resultant projects are late, or deliver less than the required functionality, IT is always to blame. Thus, the existing IT organization suffers from a lack of motivation and feeling largely unappreciated.

From the business perspective, IT does not provide what the business needs. This is largely due to the issue that business fails to communicate its needs to IT and fails to involve IT in the planning of the business. Without IT's involvement, the needs of the business are difficult to understand and, therefore, cannot be met.

The constant and continual advancement of technology results in the business wanting more and more from IT to support technology so the business can stay competitive. It is up to the IT organizations that are mature, aligned to the business, and which can consistently meet the needs of the business to ensure competitiveness of the company as a whole.

Evolving Role of IT

While IT started solely to support technology, IT doesn't just support technology any longer. If the business wanted technology, there is nothing that would keep them from acquiring their own technology. There are many computer vendors available to the business as well as to IT. In fact, the business could even go to a discount retailer and purchase a perfectly good computer along with some sodas, maybe a movie and also some dryer sheets!

The fact is, the business doesn't want technology. The business wants the service that is enabled by technology. Fortunately for IT, businesses would rather not mess with the technological issues, or the costs associated, with technology. Businesses are fine leaving the technology know-how to IT as long as they can achieve their business desired outcomes.

SERVICES AND THE DRY CLEANER

Most people have been to a dry cleaner. It is a service that we have all experienced and are familiar with. What most people do not realize, though, is everything that is involved in this seemingly simple service. As a process consultant, I am highly prone to probe behind the front counter of a service provider to better understand the steps to providing a service. The dry cleaner by my house is no exception.

When the dry cleaner first opened, I was one of their first customers. They are located in a very convenient place in my neighborhood outside of Houston, Texas and are priced reasonably. Plus, for clothes dropped off before 9:00 AM, they will be ready for pickup after 5:00 PM. That is very convenient if there is an evening event that day.

After visiting the dry cleaner on numerous occasions, I started to become curious to what actually happens at the dry cleaner after my clothes are dropped off. So, I asked the owner who gladly took me on a tour of his shop and helped me understand what it takes to get clothes cleaned and pressed.

You may think that this in no way relates to IT. However, it does.

Let's start by looking at what a dry cleaner really does. A dry cleaner provides the following services for their customers:

Cleans and presses clothes

The dry cleaner accepts soiled clothes and returns them at a later time cleaned and pressed. The returned clothes may or may not be starched, according to your desires. When returned, the clothes may be on hangers or may be boxed. When you pick up your clothes, you expect that this will be completed to your satisfaction.

Minor alterations

A dry cleaner may or may not perform minor alterations. Many dry cleaners, however, do perform minor alterations and clothing repair. These alterations may be to take in the waist on a pair of slacks, raise or lower a skirt hem, or fix buttons.

"Big" items

Periodically, we need to get our comforters, sleeping bags, and other very large items cleaned. The dry cleaner will clean these items at a higher cost, of course.

Wedding Dresses

Many dry cleaners, including the one that I frequent, will clean and pack wedding dresses in a box. This is to preserve the appearance of the dress and it is treated to prevent fading over time. With this service, you can save a wedding dress until you can pass it down to your daughter.

THE DRY CLEANING PROCESS

If you've never been in the back room of a dry cleaner to see what your clothes go through, it can be an interesting trip. Let's look at the process that your clothes go through after we arrive to drop them off.

Step 1 – Drop off

When I drop off my clothes at the dry cleaner, I put them on the counter for the clerk to count and calculate the price I pay for them to clean my clothes. Once counted, they look up my name in their computer system and input the details on my clothes. I commonly have 3 pairs of pants and 7 shirts to be cleaned. These details go into their system and a bill is produced which I have to pay when I drop off the clothes.

Step 2 – Preparation

When the bill is paid and I am given my pickup receipt, they take my clothes and put them in a cloth bag. This bag is then tied and a tag is put on the bag that identifies my clothes and keeps them separate from everyone else's. This bag is thrown into a pile with other bags until they are processed.

Step 3 – Cleaning

During the cleaning step, many bags full of clothes are placed into a washer. This washer contains a chemical that, during the wash cycle, removes the dirt and soil from the clothes. Once the clean cycle has been completed, the chemical is drained and another chemical is introduced to get rid of the first chemical. This is similar to the rinse cycle on our washing machines.

Step 4 – Drying

Once the clothes have completed the cleaning step, they are taken out of the chemical washer and placed into a dryer. The dryer then dries the chemical out of the clothes much like conventional dryers remove water out of our home laundry.

Step 5 – Sorting and Pressing

The clothes are now clean. However, they must be sorted according to customer and pressed. After the dry step, the bags of clothes are removed and placed into a bin. Individually, the bags are opened and the tag on the bag retained to identify which clothes belong to which customer.

The clothes from a bag are removed and placed on the press. At this time, starch may be added according to your specifications to stiffen the cloth in the shirts. Each item of clothing is then individually pressed and placed on a hangar. Once a certain number of items have been hung, they are covered in plastic and tagged to identify them with an individual customer. This continues until all clothes in the bag have been pressed and hung.

Step 6 – Storing

When a bag of clothes has been processed, the bundle of clothes on hangars is then placed on the clothes rack. The location of the bundle is input into the system identified by the tag number, which is linked to your customer information, and the location on the rack that the clothes are stored. You may have many bundles of clothes depending on how many items you delivered to be cleaned. These bundles are individually stored, but are referenced in the system for easy retrieval later.

Step 7 – Delivery

When you pick up your clothes at the dry cleaners, you produce a pickup receipt. This receipt identifies you as the customer and includes a list of all of the items that you dropped off. The clerk will lookup your information in their system to locate your clothes on the clothes rack. Once they get a list of all your clothing bundles, they retrieve them from the rack and deliver them to you at the front counter.

I often check to make sure that I have received all of the items that I dropped off by checking the pickup receipt to ensure that the right number of items has been returned. I also look to verify that the clothes that have been returned are actually mine. Even though other people might have better clothes than mine, I want to make sure that they fit. I've never had an issue here because their process seems to work very well, but it's always a good idea to verify that the service that you receive meets your expectations.

The sidebar example describes the process that my dry cleaner goes through to clean my clothes. This should be fairly representative of most dry cleaners as the process of cleaning clothes shouldn't change much from one dry cleaner to another.

However, this isn't all that the dry cleaner does to provide cleaning services for customers. Other things they do include the following:

Changing filters on the washer

Changing filters on the dryer

Disposing of chemical waste in a safe manner

Ordering hangars, chemicals, printer paper, plastic clothes wrap, etc.

Sweeping the floors and ensuring cleanliness of the facility

Negotiating maintenance agreements for their washers and dryers

Paying salaries

Paying utility bills such as electricity, water and gas

Finding lost clothes should a mistake be made

Completing income taxes

Complying with EPA and OSHA guidelines

Learning the latest dry cleaning techniques and applying those to their business

Many, many other things

All of these additional activities are paramount to ensuring that they provide the best possible service that they can. Without these activities being performed, the likelihood of the quality of service declining is quite high (particularly if the electricity hasn't been paid).

But, do we, as customers, care about these activities? Think about this one for a bit.

Not really. Our main desire is to get our clothes cleaned at a reasonable price. We evaluate the performance of the dry cleaner based on many factors that have very little to do with these additional activities. We base our evaluation of the dry cleaner on customer service, cleanliness of clothes, reliability, timeliness, convenience and of, course, price.

While these additional activities are important, we do not pay for them to be performed. If these activities were not performed, it would have a negative effect on the quality of the service that customers receive. This quality of service is evaluated by how clean the clothes are, whether or not we get what we pay for, whether or not our clothes are missing buttons, and other factors that have no direct relationship on these extra activities.

The key point to be made from this exercise is that *we pay for the output of this service, not the activities to provide this service.* This output represents our desired outcomes.

Now that we have explored the dry cleaner, lets turn our attention to IT. When the question of "what does IT do" is posed to IT, I often get the following responses:

> Application development
>
> Application administration
>
> Network administration
>
> Patch management
>
> Server management
>
> Vendor management
>
> Service Desk support
>
> Computer and network security
>
> Change management
>
> Desktop support
>
> IT purchasing
>
> Release management
>
> Software distribution
>
> Incident management
>
> Quality testing
>
> Quality assurance
>
> Metrics reporting
>
> Customer service management
>
> Project management

Data backup, archiving and retrieval

IT strategy and architecture

Storage

Production support

And many, many other things as well

This list of activities and responsibilities is common to almost all IT organizations with a few exceptions. Each of the items in this list is vitally important and must be performed. However, consider the following question:

As a customer, would you pay for these activities to be performed?

Absolutely not - with a few exceptions. Even though each of the items on this list is important, they do not focus on the output of a service. If any of these activities were not performed, or not performed well, the quality of the services suffer. However, these activities do not constitute a service.

The point of this story is that we judge a service and, hence, pay for it by how the service meets our business desired outcomes. The business is no different. The business would have no desire for technology if there were no business desired outcomes tied to the technology. Since business must move faster and more efficiently, there are not many options other than to utilize technology to support the desired outcomes of the business.

Instead, business wants services. The services that business wants must be aligned to their business desired outcomes in order to have any perceived value to the business. Services are focused on the value provided to the customer and include the ability to achieve those business desired outcomes (using technology) but also the design processes, transition processes, operational processes and improvement processes to support that service.

For example, business does not really want email. While every organization makes considerable use of email, email is not a service, just an application. The ability to communicate within the organization, as well as external to the organization, is the service the business wants. Today, we just happen to provide this service through email. Tomorrow, we may provide this service through some completely different mechanism (such as telepathy)!

What are Services?

A service is defined as *a means of delivering value to customers by facilitating outcomes customers want to achieve, without the ownership of specific costs and risks.*

Services have specific characteristics that include:

Services create value

Services create value of some form for the customer. If the service has no associated value, there will be no customers. The easiest way to understand this concept is to think about the services that you utilize; cable television, cell phone service, or internet services are all examples of services that create some value for you. If there was no value, you would not need the service.

Services remove the risk of ownership from customers

Customers want to achieve some outcome without being forced to own the technology, knowledge, or other underlying components that make up that service. For example, a customer wants an inventory control system in order to manage inventory. What they desire is a way to track inventory without having to understand the inventory application, installation or configuration, and without managing the server that it resides on or the network the application uses to communicate. IT provides this service, assumes ownership of these costs and maintains the required knowledge. This allows IT to share these costs among multiple customers, thus lowering individual customer costs and allowing the customer to focus on their key competencies.

Services facilitate outcomes that customers want to achieve

Services are provided to facilitate some outcome that the business desires. This business desired outcome must be well understood to ensure that the service is constructed in a way that ensures the business desired outcome is met.

Services reduce the effect of constraints

Providing services reduces the effects of constraints that may be imposed other ways. Costs, knowledge, and abilities are only a few constraints that can be reduced through the delivery of shared services.

SERVICE MANAGEMENT

Services are inherently different from other deliverables in that services have different influencers. While services come in a wide variety of forms, they all share the same characteristics of being intangible, tightly associated with customers, and being highly perishable. If services are not used, they lose their value.

Coffee beans, for example, are picked during the harvest time. The beans are then processed and stored in a manner for later use. Even though coffee beans are ultimately perishable, they have a shelf life so excess beans can be stored until needed.

Services, on the other hand, are immediately perishable. If services are not consumed at the moment they are delivered, they are wasted. Excess service cannot be stored, and high demand for services may result in the inability to meet that demand.

Because of the difference between services and other deliverables, services must be managed differently. IT Service Management (ITSM) is a collection of shared responsibilities, plus interrelated disciplines and processes that enable an organization to measure, control, and ultimately manage the IT infrastructure to deliver quality, cost-effective services to meet both short and long term business requirements. This can involve supporting one or more business areas – ranging from single application access to a complex set of facilities spread across a number of differing platforms.

Service Management is defined as *a set of specialized organizational capabilities for providing value to customers in the form of services*. Service Management is the result of focusing an organization's capabilities and resources to produce a desired outcome in the form of services. This desired outcome should meet the business needs. If appropriately focused and executed, value is created for the business.

GEPPETTO GARCIA'S GIFT CARD SERVICE

Emil Delgassi, recognizing that he needed help to realize the new gift card service that he wanted to bring to Geppetto Garcia's, went to Mark Renner, the CIO. Mark's initial impression of the idea was great. He thought that gift cards would be very well received by customers.

However, in order to ensure that both Mark and Emil were on the same page when it came to the gift cards, Mark sat down with Emil to identify what this actual service would be and what its business desired outcomes would entail.

Emil and Mark determined that the basic business desired outcome is to increase revenues and profits for individual restaurant brands by developing a new channel to reach out to customers. For the end customer, their desired outcome is to give the gift of the Geppetto Garcia dining experience.

Both Emil and Mark recognized that they would need some assistance with this project as neither of them knew exactly how the gift card service would work from a technical perspective. However, developing the definition of the service and identifying the business desired outcomes is the first step. From this definition, the guidelines are established for the rest of the work involved in establishing this service.

CHAPTER REVIEW

Definitions

Service	A means of delivering value to customers by facilitating outcomes customers want to achieve, without the ownership of specific costs and risks
Service Management	A set of specialized organizational capabilities for providing value to customers in the form of services

Characteristics of a Service

Services create value

Services remove the risk of ownership from customers

Services facilitate outcomes that customers want to achieve

CHAPTER QUIZ

1. _____ create value, remove risk of ownership from customers, facilitate outcomes customers want to achieve and reduce the effect of constraints

   a. Resources
   b. Services
   c. New Components
   d. Sales

2. What are the differentiators of a service?

   a. Tightly coupled with the customer's assets
   b. Intangible
   c. Perishable
   d. Speed

3. _____ is a set of specialized organizational capabilities for providing value to customers in the form of services.

   a. Service Management
   b. Information Technology
   c. The art of service
   d. Services

CHAPTER QUIZ ANSWERS

1.   B
2.   A, B, C
3.   A

Introduction to ITIL®

Good Practices

Good practices are practices that are commonly used within an organization. Good practices are often derived from best practices until they are commonly performed and become a commodity. At this point, they become good practice. Good practices are validated across a diverse set of environments and are critiqued in more than just a single organization.

ITIL® is an example of best practice becoming good practice. While ITIL® started as a library of defined best practices, it has been reviewed, tried and validated across a diverse set of organizations. This use of ITIL® has resulted in it becoming a good practice that IT organizations can adopt.

ITIL® is the combined result of people around the world that have been tasked with documenting their best practice experiences. The contributors to the IT Infrastructure Library have vast experience in a wide variety of industries and organizations.

What is ITIL®?

I affectionately refer to ITIL® as "documented common sense." It is my contention that any organization with enough vision, forethought, time, need, and desire would come up with almost all of the things that ITIL® documents. The organization may use different words to mean the same things as in ITIL®, but the ideas would be there.

The IT Infrastructure Library (ITIL®) is simply a set of practices that people just like you have documented because they work well. ITIL® is not prescriptive in that it does not document how to do things. It simply documents what can and should be done. Along with the ITIL® core library is supplemental information that provides more prescriptive guidance, but overall, ITIL® simply shares with us what other people have found to be the best way to approach IT as a service provider.

The Office of Government Commerce (OGC) is an office of the British HM Treasury that currently owns the rights to ITIL®. ITIL® was originally developed in the mid-1980's by the Central Computer and Telecommunications Agency (CCTA), in collaboration with subject matter experts, practitioners, consultants, and trainers to help organizations improve the way we use and manage IT. The CCTA is now incorporated into the OGC and does not operate as a separate entity.

The OGC now has the authority for maintenance and improvement of ITIL®, as well as implementing the best practices in commercial activities in the UK's government. The OGC continues to build on this practice by working with international organizations to develop and share business and practitioner guidance to further enhance this world-class best practice.

ITIL® v3

The current version, ITIL® version 3, was introduced in June, 2007. This version of ITIL® had the involvement of the IT Service Management Forum (ITSMF). The ITSMF is a worldwide forum involved in promoting the concepts of IT Service Management and organizing events and conferences to bring IT Service Management practitioners together. The ITSMF US chapter can be found on the web at www.itsmfusa.org. The ITSMF also promotes Local Interest Groups (LIGs) for those that want to meet on a regular basis in the cities in which they live or work. LIGs for your area can also be found on the ITSMF US web site.

ITIL® AND OTHER STANDARDS

ITIL® is not an exclusive framework. ITIL® documents "what" a mature IT organization should do, not "how" it should do it. Other standards still play a very important part in maturing an IT organization. In particular, ISO 20000 is the ISO certification for organizations around ITIL®. Also, ITIL® is a requirement in order to achieve BS15000 certification for an organization.

ITIL® has been around since 1986 when the first version was introduced. Over the past 20+ years, ITIL® has evolved as the de facto standard in IT Service Management. The latest version of ITIL®, v3, was delivered in 2007. This latest version expands on what we learned in ITIL® v2 and introduces the Service Lifecycle.

THE ITIL® CORE

A service, much like an application, has a lifecycle with defined stages during the life of the service. The Service Lifecycle defines five key stages within this lifecycle; Service Strategy, Service Design, Service Transition, Service Operation and Continual Service Improvement. These Service Lifecycle stages work together to provide a complete service from conception through retirement of the service.

ITIL® version 3 consists of 5 core volumes that document these Service Lifecycle stages: Service Strategy, Service Design, Service Transition, Service Operation and Continual Service Improvement. The ITIL® v3 core volumes were published in June, 2007. In September, 2007, the "Official Introduction to ITIL®" was published. This volume introduces ITIL® and the Service Lifecycle.

ITIL® v3 is supplemented with complementary guidance that documents specific best practices by industry and by organization. Additional publications are being made available through the continued effort of people around the world as they document various aspects of ITIL®. These additional publications are available through the ITIL® v3 web site at www.best-management-practice.com.

Service Lifecycle

ITIL® approaches the practice of Service Management through a framework called the Service Lifecycle. The Service Lifecycle represents the stages that a service goes through during its life.

ITIL® documents the stages of the Service Lifecycle based on the input from people all over the world in various industries. This library provides guidance for the practice of IT Service Management.

5 Core Volumes

The ITIL® core is a set of books that provide guidance for each of the stages of the Service Lifecycle. These core volumes follow each stage of the Service Lifecycle by documenting the lifecycle stage objectives, concepts and the processes within each stage of the Service Lifecycle.

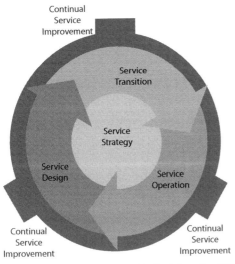

©Crown copyright 2007 - Reproduced under license from OGC

Figure 2 - Service Lifecycle

Service Strategy

The Service Strategy volume provides guidance in developing an overall strategy for IT Service Management. This involves understanding your markets, your customers, your capabilities and resources, and the financial constraints under which these services must be defined, delivered and supported. Service Strategy also includes the ongoing processes of Portfolio Management, Financial Management and Demand Management.

The overall purpose of Service Strategy is to develop a strategy for our specific markets (customers) based on services that result in the IT organization being non-optional. The IT organization should be the best option as a "vendor" of services that understands the requirements and delivers services which are superior to any other vendor.

Service Design

The Service Design volume provides guidance on the principles of balancing design against a diverse set of constraints. It also discussed how to design a service that meets the business needs, is financially justifiable, and can be supported as an ongoing concern. Service Design incorporates these requirements into a set of design documents upon which a service, or modification to a service, can be developed.

Service Transition

The Service Transition volume provides guidance on the transitioning of a service into operation. Service Transition considers all elements required for a service. These elements include all aspects of a service, both technical and non-technical. This holistic view of a service helps to ensure that the service is transitioned in a way that it can be supported as an ongoing concern as effectively and efficiently as possible.

Service Operation

The Service Operation volume provides guidance on the effective and efficient operation of the service. Service Operation is where the value of the service is realized and the strategy of the organization is executed. Service Operation is important to Continual Service Improvement as the Service Operation stage is where the services are monitored and improvements are identified.

Continual Service Improvement

The Continual Service Improvement (CSI) volumes provide guidance that ensures improvements to a service are diligently executed. Continual Service Improvement is defined in such a way that it should be integrated into all of the other lifecycle stages. The CSI volume describes improvement as a continual activity and not just an afterthought.

As you will learn, the outputs of one stage of the Service Lifecycle become inputs into another. Continual Service Improvement outputs are inputs to all other Service Lifecycle stages.

Chapter Summary

Good practices are validated across a diverse set of environments and are critiqued in more than just a single organization.

The Office of Government Commerce (OGC) currently owns the rights to ITIL®

ISO 20000 is the ISO certification for organizations around ITIL®.

ITIL® is a requirement in order to achieve BS15000 certification for an organization.

ITIL Core Volumes

Service Strategy

The Service Strategy volume provides guidance in developing an overall strategy for IT Service Management.

Service Design

The Service Design volume provides guidance on the principles of balancing design against a diverse set of constraints.

Service Transition

The Service Transition volume provides guidance on the transitioning of a service into operation.

Service Operation

The Service Operation volume provides guidance on the effective and efficient operation of the service.

Continual Service Improvement

The Continual Service Improvement (CSI) volume provides guidance that ensures improvements to a service are diligently executed.

Chapter Quiz

1. What does ITIL stand for?

    a. Information Technology Information Language
    b. Information Technology Infrastructure Lessons
    c. Information Technology Infrastructure Library
    d. It's Too Inane to Last

2. Why might an organization want to use ITIL?

    a. ITIL is published good practice
    b. ITIL provides a standard upon which to compare
    c. ITIL provides a basis on which to improve
    d. ITIL is a validated framework
    e. All of the above

3. Which of the following own the rights to ITIL?

    a. OGC
    b. ITSMF
    c. PMI
    d. Nobody owns the rights to ITIL

4. Which ISO standard is based on ITIL?

    a. ISO 20001
    b. ISO 20000
    c. There is no ISO support for ITIL
    d. ISO 9000

5.

ITIL is a standalone, totally inclusive framework which eliminates the need to consider any other standard.

    a.   True

    b.   False

6.   What are the ITIL core volumes in order?

    a.   Service Strategy, Service Design, Continual Service Improvement, Service Transition, Service Operation

    b.   Service Operation, Service Strategy, Service Design, Continual Service Improvement, Service Transition

    c.   Service Transition, Service Operation, Service Design, Continual Service Improvement, Service Strategy

    d.   Service Strategy, Service Design, Service Transition, Service Operation, Continual Service Improvement

Answers

1. C
2. E
3. A
4. B
5. B
6. D

Processes, Functions and Roles

Overview

IT Service Management is made possible through a combination of functions and processes. A process is defined as *a structured set of activities designed to accomplish a specific set of objectives* while a function is defined as *units of organizations specialized to perform certain types of work and responsible for specific outcomes.* Processes are performed by functions providing coordination across the functions.

Processes

Geppetto Garcia quickly realized that in order to serve his customers well, he needed to develop processes to prepare meals for his customers. The kitchen staff worked with Geppetto to develop processes to support preparing meals. For Chicken Parmigiana, for example, the process consists of a number of steps with defined procedures.

The basic process for preparing Chicken Parmigiana consists of the following steps:

1. Bread chicken
2. Cook chicken
3. Spoon marinara sauce onto plate
4. Place cooked chicken on plate

5. Place Parmesan cheese on chicken

6. Place plate in oven to melt cheese

7. Add spaghetti noodles to plate

8. Spoon sauce over spaghetti noodles

A process consists of a set of activities that build upon each other until a specific outcome is achieved. Each specific outcome is individually countable. In the above case, the specific outcome is a Chicken Parmigiana meal. By counting the specific outcomes, the number of Chicken Parmigiana meals prepared can be counted.

Each specific outcome is delivered to a customer of the process. The customer of the process does not have to be the end consumer of the output of the process. Often times, the outputs of the process are inputs into another process. In this case, the customer of the Chicken Parmigiana process is the server. The server will then deliver the meal to the customer.

The process does not start until a triggering event occurs to start the process activities. In our case, a meal is ordered and an order is sent to the kitchen. This specific event (an order) begins the process of creating a Chicken Parmigiana meal.

Processes are also measurable. Because they are measurable, they are performance driven. With a process, we can tell how long it takes to perform the process and even how long it

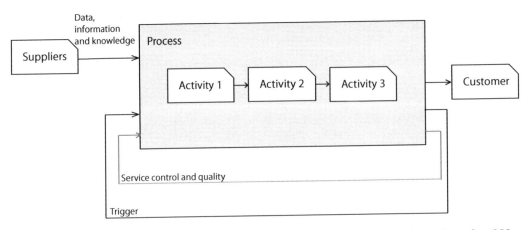

©Crown copyright 2007 - Reproduced under license from OGC

Figure 3 - Basic Closed Loop Process

takes to perform the individual activities within the process. In our example, the time it takes to prepare a Chicken Parmigiana meal should be well known so if a table of diners orders different meals, each of the meals can be started at a time when they can all be completed at the same time to be delivered to the process customer (the server) together.

Processes have no staff or defined organization; they are simply sets of activities. They act on a defined triggering event (input) to provide some defined output. Processes have roles, responsibilities, and tools and require management control to ensure that the output is delivered reliably. Processes also define policies, standards, guidelines, activities and work instructions that govern them. Lastly, processes are closed loop systems that provide feedback for corrective action to be applied.

For the exam, remember that processes must be Measurable, have a Specific output, deliver to a Customer, and Respond to a trigger. The term MaSsaCRe may help remember this.

> M – Measurable
>
> S – Specific output
>
> C – Customer
>
> R – Respond to a trigger

When designing a process, it's not wise to focus on designing a perfect process, but a process with built-in improvement mechanisms for long-term improvement. This is accomplished through Process Control that measures, evaluates, and continually improves the process. Process Control is defined as *the process of planning and regulating, with the objective of performing a process in an effective, efficient and objective manner*.

Even though processes do not define organizations or people, many times we will refer to processes as if they were actual organizations or individuals. For example, Incident Management passes information to Problem Management. This example appears as if different people are involved in this hand-off of information. In fact, the opposite is true – processes have no organization or staff. In this example, when information passes from Incident Management to Problem Management, it is likely that the information will be passed by a single individual without them realizing that they are changing from one process to another.

Be sure to keep this in mind through the remainder of this course. Processes do not describe organizations.

FUNCTIONS

Functions are defined as *units of organizations specialized to perform certain types of work and responsible for specific outcomes*. In Geppetto Garcia's restaurant, the kitchen staff is an example of a function. The kitchen staff is an organization and they are trained to perform specialized types of work (cook). They are also responsible for specific outcomes (the individual meals).

In your organization, you also have functions of many types. Examples of functions include the Service Desk or Help Desk staff, the Technical Management teams, the Application Management teams and the IT Operations Management teams. These specific functions are addressed in the Service Operation Functions chapter.

Functions have the characteristics of organizations that are self-contained, have specific resources and capabilities, provide performance and outcomes, have their own body of knowledge (usually procedures), provide structure and stability to an organization and have defined roles and associated authority.

In the coming pages of the book, specific processes and their activities will be explored. It is common to wonder who performs all of these activities. It is the functions that perform these activities within the processes. The processes provide a mechanism for the functions to work together to provide a service. By using processes for coordination, functions can be very powerful.

ROLES

Within each process that we will explore, roles are documented. These roles define the responsibilities that this role performs.

For example, Geppetto Garcia is a restaurateur. He is also a friend, and a son. On his days off, he enjoys playing chess in the park. Geppetto Garcia has many roles (restaurateur, friend, son, chess player), but he is only one person. You, the reader, also have many roles. You are an employee, a friend, a son or daughter, and you may also be a mom or a dad. From this, can see that each one of us has multiple roles.

Therefore, a role does not define an individual. A role is simply a set of responsibilities that are performed. A role may be combined with other roles so one person can assume multiple roles. Also, a role may be shared, so more than one person can assume this role.

In the following chapters, you will learn about specific roles for the processes within the Service Lifecycle. However, there are some generic roles described by ITIL. These roles are generic and more specific descriptions may be provided later.

Every process should have a Process Owner and a Process Manager. The Process Owner is defined as *the role responsible for ensuring that a process is fit for purpose.* The Process Owner is also responsible for the sponsorship of the process, ensuring the process is designed, and also responsible to identify opportunities for improvement.

The Process Manager is defined as *the role responsible for the operational management of a process.* The Process Manager ensures that a process operates as expected and identifies areas of potential improvements to effectiveness and efficiency. The Process Manager also plans and coordinates the activities of the process, and is responsible for the monitoring and reporting of a process.

The Service Owner is defined as *the role responsible to the customer for the initiation, transition and ongoing maintenance and support of a particular service.* The Service Owner is the main contact person for a specific service to ensure that the service is meeting its objectives for the customer. The Service Owner also establishes and maintains relationships with Process Owners and Process Managers throughout the Service Lifecycle to ensure the service is well designed, meets the strategy, is transitioned well, is effectively and efficiently operated and is continually improved to meet the business needs.

Larger organizations may have several Process Managers for one process. This is particularly true for distributed organizations by having one Process Manager per region. However, there is only one Process Owner per process. Smaller organizations may combine the roles of Process Manager and Process Owner so one person assumes both roles.

Two other roles that are defined are customers and users. A Customer is defined as *the person or group who defines and agrees the Service Level Targets.* The Customer is the person who represents the business interests. The Customer is the person who "pays" for the service or negotiates the service on behalf of the business and the users. Users are the people who use the service on a day-to-day basis.

RACI Model

Identification of specific roles and responsibilities are made easier through the development of a RACI Model. A RACI Model identifies those who are Responsible, Accountable, Consulted and Informed (RACI) for the specific activities in a process.

Responsibility refers to the resource that carries out a task to completion. Responsibility may be shared among multiple people.

Accountability refers the person that is ultimately responsible for the success or failure of the task. This role has decision making power regarding the activity. There can be only one person accountable for a specific task. If there is more than one person accountable for a task, then when the task fails, finger-pointing occurs and, as a result, no one is accountable. I can think of many examples of this that has occurred in my career and I'm sure you can probably think of examples, as well.

Consulted refers to the resources that must be conferred with regarding a task or activity. Consulted involves a two way communication with those conferred. For example, if a change must be made to a service, the Change Manager may want to consult with the business customers of that service to determine when the change can be made.

Informed refers to communicating one-way. Informing is simply communicating that something is taking place with no expectation of a response. For example, once the Change Manager determines when a change can be made, the Change Manager may inform the users of that service that the change is being made and when.

A RACI Model is developed by listing the activities along the left column of a table and the roles across the top. A matrix is then developed to identify which roles are responsible, accountable, consulted or informed within the process.

	Change Requestor	Change Manager	Change Approver	Change Implementor	Change Tester
Request a Change	R	A			
Filter the Change		R/A		C	
Approve the Change		A	R		
Build the Change		A		R	I
Implement the Change		A		R	C
Test the Change		A		C	R
Review the Change	C	R/A		C	C
Close the Change	I	R/A	I	I	I

R - Responsible
A - Accountable
C - Consulted
I - Informed

©Crown copyright 2007 - Reproduced under license from OGC

Figure 4 - RACI Model

A RACI Model ensures that end-to-end accountability is identified for the process activities and ensures that gaps are identified and can be corrected.

A RACI Model has potential problems that should be understood. Within the RACI Model, a process can only have one person accountable. Sharing accountability can result in finger pointing, resulting in no accountability. The RACI model should also ensure that the responsibilities for closely related processes are properly identified to ensure that the process relationships remain intact.

Processes, in general, have the issue that responsibility may be delegated, but this delegation results in no authority to make decisions. Also, individual agendas or goals may get in the way of satisfying the overall goals of the process. Process interrelationships must also be considered so that there is defined interaction and, perhaps, shared responsibility between activities of highly related processes.

CHAPTER REVIEW

Definitions

Process	A structured set of activities designed to accomplish a specific set of objectives
Function	Units of organizations specialized to perform certain types of work and responsible for specific outcomes
Process Control	The process of planning and regulating with the objective of performing a process in an effective, efficient and objective manner

Characteristics of a Process

Measurable

Specific output

Customer

Respond to a trigger

Characteristics of a Function

Self-contained units of organization

Has specific resources and capabilities

Provide performance and outcomes

Have own body of knowledge

Provide structure and stability to an organization

Have defined roles and associated authority

Roles

Process Owner	The role responsible for ensuring that a process is fit for purpose
Process Manager	The role responsible for the operational management of a process

Service Owner The role responsible to the customer for the initiation, transition and ongoing maintenance and support of a particular service

Customer The person or group who defines and agrees the Service Level Targets

Users The people who use the service on a day-to-day basis

RACI Model

Identifies those who are Responsible, Accountable, Consulted and Informed (RACI) for the specific activities in a process.

CHAPTER QUIZ

1. There are times when it is feasible to have more than one person accountable for a process.

    a. True
    b. False

2. Match the following roles:

    a. Responsible for ensuring that a process is fit for purpose
    b. Responsible for the operational management of a process
    c. Responsible to the customer for the ongoing maintenance and support of a specific service

    i. Process Owner
    ii. Service Owner
    iii. Process Manager

3. Functions have an organizational structure.

    a. True
    b. False

4. The process of planning and regulating, with the objective of performing a process in an effective, efficient and objective manner is:

    a. Activity Control
    b. Service Management
    c. Process Control
    d. Process Management

5. The characteristics of a process include:

    a.   Responds to a specific event (trigger)

    b.   It is timely

    c.   It is supported by a single function

    d.   It is measurable

    e.   It has a specific output

    f.   It provides a specific output to a customer

    g.   It is efficient and effective

6. _____ are units of organizations specialized to perform certain types of work and responsible for specific outcomes.

    a.   Work orders

    b.   Processes

    c.   Divisions

    d.   Functions

7. Processes have an organizational structure.

    a.   True

    b.   False

8. A RACI Model is used to identify what?

    a.   Who is responsible

    b.   Who is accountable

    c.   Who is consulted

    d.   Who pays for the project

    e.   Who is informed

9. Delegating responsibility for a process without delegating authority to make decisions is a common problem with processes.

    a. True
    b. False

10. _____ are a structured set of activities designed to accomplish a specific set of objectives.

    a. Courses
    b. Processes
    c. Functions
    d. Work Orders

Answers

1. B
2. A – i, B – iii, C – ii
3. A
4. C
5. A, D, E, F
6. D
7. B
8. A, B, C, E
9. A
10. B

5

SERVICE STRATEGY OVERVIEW

OVERVIEW

In this chapter, the concepts of Service Strategy are described. The Service Strategy volume is largely intended for IT executives. However, it is still important that while learning about IT Service Management, you understand the basics of Service Strategy. It is important for everyone to understand why and how decisions are made. A common issue with a job of any type, not just IT, is understanding the big picture. The Service Strategy volume provides the big picture and describes how each of us is involved in providing services to customers.

Upon completing this chapter, you will understand the basics of Service Strategy as part of the Service Lifecycle. You will also have an understanding of value creation through services, as well as concepts in designing services.

GEPPETTO GARCIA'S

Geppetto Garcia's began expanding across the United States. During their expansion, they recognized the need to develop standards that would drive consistency across their restaurants regardless of the location or specific cuisine of the restaurant. To achieve this consistency, Geppetto developed a strategy that would centralize the provisioning of his restaurants, including maintaining quality standards, inventory control, Human Resources, Accounting, maintaining suppliers, and providing IT services.

The restaurant business, just like almost any other business of reasonable size, requires the use of IT. Geppetto Garcia hired Mark Renner to be the Chief Information Officer (CIO) of Geppetto Garcia, Inc.

Mark realized that in order to meet Geppetto's high quality and consistency standards, he would need to develop standard and consistent IT services that could be provisioned for each restaurant. These IT services would address the areas of inventory control, the restaurant ordering and payment systems, and employee time scheduling. Centralized services for the corporate facilities would involve email services, Human Resources, Finance, Sales and Marketing and overall operations.

Mark realized that he had two major markets to focus on – the individual restaurants, as well as his corporate services. These markets are two distinct markets with differing needs. His first focus is on ensuring the overall business revenue can be maintained. Therefore, he focused on the restaurant market first.

To identify the needs of the services, the customer of that service must first be identified. The restaurants are under the direction of the Chief Operating Officer, Emil Delgassi. Emil's staff includes the Vice President in charge of restaurant operations, Genevieve Boswell. Mark contacted Genevieve to discuss the specific needs of the services that her restaurants would require from corporate IT in order to function effectively.

Mark documented these requirements in a Service Portfolio. The Service Portfolio matches the individual business requirements to services identified in the Service Portfolio. From this list of requirements, Mark defined specific services that meet these requirements. These services include specific services for Inventory Control, Employee Time Scheduling, and Ordering and Payment services.

Based on the specific services that Mark would offer to the restaurants, he then went to work building the things that he would need to provide these services including hardware and software, people, tools to measure and maintain the services, and processes to ensure that these services would operate effectively and efficiently, as well as be readily maintained. These things required for the service are called Service Assets.

Mark next developed a plan to prepare for execution of these services. To do this, he evaluated internal and external factors, developed a plan for specific actions, developed policies and procedures to support his plan, and then enacted his plan. His plan involved ensuring that the specific services supplied would be of high enough quality to meet the demand for the services, as well as be financially viable. His overall goal was not to provide the highest quality services, but to provide the right level of service at the right cost.

The services that Mark identified which needed to be developed included Inventory

Control, Employee Time Scheduling, and Ordering and Payment Services. He also understands that each of these services must have an identified customer and someone who "owns" the service and can represent IT's capabilities to the customer as well as represent the business requirements to IT. This person is called a Service Owner. From his IT and Business Analyst staff, he identified three individuals to become the Service Owners for each of these services.

Mark developed the following table that specified the service, the primary customer and Service Owner.

Service	Description	Service Owner	Customer
Inventory Control	Ensures materials and supplies are delivered to individual restaurants based on consumption rates of stocked materials and supplies	Dina Williams	Genevieve Boswell – VP, Operations
Employee Time Scheduling	Supports scheduling of restaurant employees to maintain the proper level of staffing matched to anticipated demand.	Robin Jackson, IT	Brenda Fuller – Director, Time Management (HR)
Ordering and Payment Services	Automates the ordering of meals from diners and prioritizes workflow within the kitchen. Provides diner checks for payment.	Russell Diamond	Alan Hamilton – VP, Finance

PURPOSE OF SERVICE STRATEGY

In order to operate and grow successfully in the long-term, service providers must have the ability to think and act in a strategic manner. Service Strategy describes the strategic decisions that are made regarding services and IT Service Management. Through these strategic decisions, IT can drive value to the business through its effective application of capabilities and resources.

IT organizations were originally established to provide technical services to the business. Today, with the complexity of IT and the dependency of business on technology, IT has, or should, evolve to a service provider. In order to become a service provider, IT must understand the business aspects of providing service. By doing this, IT will become more competitive, more focused, and become the preferred "vendor" of IT services to the business.

More than just technical expertise is required to achieve this level. It involves a multi-disciplinary approach that utilizes knowledge in the areas of Organizational Management, Marketing, Sales, Systems Dynamics, and many other areas. These areas are usually not taught to IT people. However, they are critical to IT Service Providers.

The major output of Service Strategy is the Service Level Package (SLP). The SLP documents the business requirements for a service along with guiding constraints, process requirements and other requirements for the service. The SLP serves as an input to the Service Design stage of the Service Lifecycle.

CREATING VALUE THROUGH SERVICES

As discussed earlier, services create value for the customer. This value is created through the effective use of service assets. A Service Asset is defined as *any capability or resource of a Service Provider.*

Capabilities consist of the "soft assets" of an organization including:

> Management
>
> Organization
>
> Processes
>
> Knowledge
>
> People

Capabilities are the things we know and how we do things in order to accomplish a goal.

Resources are the "hard assets" of the organization including:

> Financial Capital
>
> Infrastructure
>
> Applications
>
> Information
>
> People

Resources are investments we make and the "components" that we use to get things done. Note that people are both capabilities and resources of a Service Asset. The way we get things done is through people and we make an investment in people.

If value is created, the result will be that there are no other options for the business other than the IT organization. This makes the IT organization as a Service Provider non-optional.

There is nothing that you can put your hands on and say "this is the service that we provide." Service is a human concept that is made up of the 4 P's – People, Processes, Partners (vendors) and Products (Technology). The products are the last and the least important of these 4 P's. If all the business wanted was technology (products), they could easily purchase it themselves. However, the business desires a service to help them meet their business desired objectives.

Key Point: IT does NOT exist to provide technology. IT exists to provide services.

Defining a service requires understanding the business desired outcomes of customers. It is these business desired outcomes that the service is designed to satisfy. Without this understanding, the service's value to the customer is minimized. Understanding the business desired outcomes requires knowledge other than engineering or technical. It requires the ability to communicate with the customer in terms that the business understands, which means we must have knowledge of not only the business but also Sales, Marketing, Economics and other business-oriented disciplines.

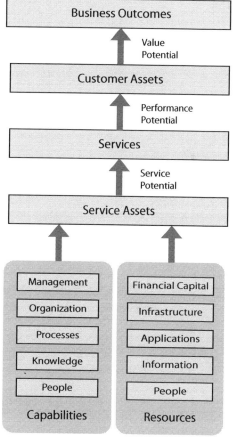

©Crown copyright 2007 - Reproduced under license from OGC

Figure 5 - Creating Value

If we describe a service in terms of technology (the traditional view of IT), we lose our ability to communicate with the business and thus reduce the value of IT. In short, the business doesn't care about the technology, only about your ability to meet their business desired outcomes.

The other side effect of being too focused on technology is communications. IT most often solves problems in terms of technology. Therefore, the communications is always technology related. Because of this focus on technology, the business is forced to commu-

SharePoint Proliferation

One of my pharmaceutical clients related a story to me about SharePoint servers. When SharePoint first came out, the IT department was trying them out for their own purposes. One of IT's customers observed an IT staff member working on a SharePoint server and inquired about it. Once the customer realized some of the things they could do with SharePoint, they asked for a SharePoint server.

The IT staff member, anxious to show off their knowledge of the inner workings of technology, fulfilled that request and set up a SharePoint server for the customer. Soon after that, other customers were asking for SharePoint servers as well. This caused the proliferation of SharePoint servers throughout the organization. This, by itself, is not a bad thing. Technology is there to help people be more productive. These SharePoint servers were playing their part in the productivity of the business.

One afternoon, one of the SharePoint servers suffered a catastrophic failure. This server crashed in a manner that no data was recoverable and the entire server was scrapped. A new SharePoint server was set up for the business as a result of the failure.

However, the business wasn't satisfied with a new server. They wanted their

nicate with IT in terms of technology – terms that IT understands – instead of the business desired outcomes. Often, this leads to engineering solutions for the business that fail to meet the business desired outcomes.

The story in the sidebar reveals some interesting things about how IT should approach their solutions to the business. Even though the business request would have probably been provided through the use of a SharePoint server, the business perspective of IT would have increased dramatically if IT would have taken the time to provide a true service, instead of technology. Service Strategy assists with this communication by asking "why" we do things before "how" we do them.

Service Strategy strives to help IT understand the business perspective of IT in order for IT to be more successful in providing value to their customers. This change of perspective is paramount for IT to advance beyond a technology provider. In the future, companies with IT organizations that have this perspective will be the most successful.

Value of Services

While services provide and communicate value, value can be a subjective thing. Depending on the person, an old table may be a piece of junk or it may be a priceless antique. Value is determined by the customer's perception, preferences, and business outcomes. Understanding how value perspective is determined is critical to providing that value.

This perspective is defined in part by perception.

A customer's perception is influenced by their experiences, what competitors are doing and their own self image. For example, a customer may be a risk taker or risk adverse. Risk taking customers may be open to using new technologies and services that are cutting edge. Risk adverse customers may want to use technologies and services that are very stable and not cutting edge. Understanding what drives the customer's perception is important because the service that is provided may not be perceived as adding value – due entirely to the customer's perception.

Customers also have preferences. These preferences may be driven by past experiences or impressions, among other things. We all have preferences. These preferences may have no reason, other than they are our preferences. If we all had the same preferences, we would all be driving the same model and color car.

Business outcomes also drive value perspective. A service must enable business outcomes to be achieved or no value will be delivered to the customer.

data back. IT could not provide this request because the data was gone. The business had stored all of their project related documents, research and design documents and patent applications on this SharePoint server. All of that work had to be re-created.

This was a big blow to IT in terms of perceived value. While IT provided exactly what the business asked for, they failed to understand the business desired outcomes and reasons for requesting a SharePoint server. Had IT taken the time to really understand the customer needs for a collaboration environment instead of a SharePoint server, they would have provided the entire service, including backup and restore, to meet this legitimate need.

DEFINING A SERVICE

Customers do not buy services for the sake of the service. They buy the ability to achieve their business desired outcome.

Services are described in terms of utility and warranty. Utility is defined as *the functionality offered of a product or service to meet a particular need (what it does or fit for purpose)*. Warranty is defined as *a promise or guarantee that a product or service will meet its requirements (how well it does it or fit for use)*.

The utility of a service supports performance of a customer and removes constraints from customers. The warranty of a service refers to the availability, capacity, continuity and security of a service.

When defining services in Service Strategy, the following questions should strive to be answered:

> What is our business?
>
> Who is our customer?
>
> What does the customer value?
>
> Who depends on our services?
>
> How do they use our services?
>
> Why are they valuable to them?

These questions are answered by Service Strategy. During the chapter on the shared Service Strategy activities, you will find that these shared activities are focused precisely on these questions and how to satisfy the requirements of the customer.

TYPES OF SERVICES

When considering services, there are different types. Some services directly support the business desired outcomes of the customer. These services are called core services. Other services do not directly provide the business desired outcomes of the customer, but support the services that do. These services enable or enhance a core service. These types of services are called supporting services. Combinations of core services and supporting services are called service packages.

For example, when you visit an ATM machine, your basic desire is to obtain cash. Suppose on your trip to the ATM, the machine is not able to print a receipt, but can still dispense cash. You will probably still use the ATM machine because your desired outcome is to walk away with cash in your pocket. The ability to dispense cash is the core service. Printing the receipt is a supporting service as it enhances the overall service. The ATM machine, with the ability to dispense cash and print a receipt, is the service package.

Supporting services both enable and enhance. Enhancement is adding value to a service above and beyond the core service, such as printing a receipt at an ATM machine. Enabling services are usually services that the customer does not see, such as the communications service. Without the communications service, the ATM does not function. However, the customer rarely knows that this service exists.

Other supporting enabling services for the ATM machine include the network ser-

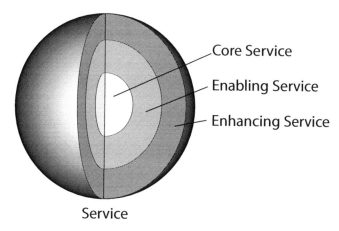

Core Service

Enabling Service

Enhancing Service

Service

Figure 6 - Core, Enabling and Enhancing Services

vices for communication, the electricity to power the ATM machine as well as security services such as the lighting and security cameras. Supporting enhancing services for an ATM may be the ability to sell postage stamps, paying bills and making deposits.

A Service Package is defined as *a detailed description of an IT service that is available to be delivered to customers.*

The core service is defined as *a service that delivers basic outcomes desired by one or more customers.*

The supporting service is defined as *a service that enables or enhances a core service.*

Chapter Review

Definitions

Service Asset	Any capability or resource of a Service Provider
Utility	The functionality offered of a product or service to meet a particular need (what it does or fit for purpose)
Warranty	A promise or guarantee that a product or service will meet its requirements (how well it does it or fit for use)
Service Package	A detailed description of an IT service that is available to be delivered to customers
Core Service	A service that delivers basic outcomes desired by one or more customers
Supporting Service	A service that enables or enhances a core service

Capabilities - "soft assets" of the organization

Management

Organization

Processes

Knowledge

People

Resources - "hard assets" of the organization

Financial Capital

Infrastructure

Applications

Information

People

Service Strategy

Purpose

Provide guidance for service providers to think and act in a strategic manner.

Major Output

Service Level Package (SLP)

CHAPTER QUIZ

1. Service Strategy drives value though the effective application of capabilities and resources.

    a. True
    b. False

2. The _____ is the major output of Service Strategy.

    a. Service Level Package
    b. Service Management Package
    c. Service Design Package
    d. Service Strategy Package

3. Services deliver what?

    a. Business desired outcomes
    b. Value
    c. Resource justification
    d. Satisfied customers

4. Service Assets consist of _____ and _____.

    a. Functions
    b. Capabilities
    c. Processes
    d. Resources

5. Which of the following are capabilities?

    a. People

    b. Infrastructure

    c. Processes

    d. Financial Capital

    e. Organization

    f. Information

    g. Management

    h. Knowledge

    i. Applications

6. Which of the following are resources?

    a. Knowledge

    b. Processes

    c. Financial Capital

    d. Applications

    e. Infrastructure

    f. Information

    g. Management

    h. Organization

    i. People

7. Match the concepts with their meanings.

    a. Utility – What is does (Fit for purpose)

    b. Warranty – What it does (Fit for purpose)

    c. Utility – How well it does it (Fit for use)

    d. Warranty – How well it does it (Fit for use)

8. Experience, competitors, and self-image all influence the _____ of service.

    a. Usefulness

    b. Utility

    c. Perception

    d. Warranty

    e. Value

9. _____ Is the functionality offered of a product or service to meet a particular need.

    a. Utility

    b. Warranty

    c. Capacity

    d. None of the above

10. _____ is the promise or guarantee that a product or service will meet its requirements.

    a. Utility

    b. Warranty

    c. Capacity

    d. None of the above

Answers

1. A
2. A
3. B
4. B, D
5. A, C, E, G, H
6. C, D, E, F, I
7. A, D
8. E
9. A
10. B

6

Service Design Overview

Overview

This chapter provides an overview of the Service Design stage of the Service Lifecycle. In this chapter, you will learn the purpose, objectives and value to business of Service Design, as well as the key concepts of the value of design, sourcing options, and the Service Knowledge Management System (SKMS).

Service Design takes the requirements contained within the Service Level Package (SLP) from Service Strategy to design a service, or a change to a service, to meet those requirements. When designing a service, Service Design takes into account all of the elements of that service, not just the technical solution. The design of that service also includes the design of knowledge, processes, measurements, and Service Management tools and processes. This design is included in the major output of Service Design, the Service Design Package (SDP).

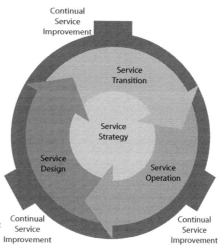

©Crown copyright 2007 - Reproduced under license from OGC

Figure 7 - Service Lifecycle

GEPPETTO GARCIA'S GIFT CARD SERVICE

In order to design a service for the ability to process gift cards, Mark Renner recognizes that the IT systems, in particular the retail systems, must change in order to facilitate this new service. However, the technology is only part of the considerations in the design. For this service to provide the most value possible to the restaurants and to the diners, all aspects of this service must be designed.

Mark again met with Emil Delgassi, the Chief Operating Officer for Geppetto Garcia's. Together, they determined all of the aspects of this service that need to be considered as part of the design.

First, they needed to determine what options they had for procurement of the gift cards. They listed the possibilities that they could produce the gift cards themselves, or purchase them from a company that specializes in gift cards. When the consideration of involving an outside organization came up, they determined that they needed to inquire about additional services that a company that specializes in gift cards might provide. An external company may better understand how to market, distribute, and manage the selling of gift cards because they may have established channels into the market already.

Another aspect of their design was the processes that need to be developed or changed to support gift cards. The retail systems need to be modified to accept and sell gift cards. However, other processes need to be addressed as well, such as training on how to accept a gift card from a customer and the accounting processes needed to address this new source of purchasing from diners. Therefore, training was added to part of the design of the service.

While reviewing their definition of the business desired outcome, to increase revenue and profits for the restaurants, Emil and Mark discussed how to ensure that their business desired outcomes are being achieved. They determined that they needed a way to measure gift card sales and redemptions to ensure that the business desired objectives were being met. Therefore, they added metrics and measurements of the service to part of the design.

Gift cards, just like any other form of electronic fund transfer, requires technology to support it. Mark, being responsible for the Information Technology organization, agreed to address the technology requirements that would be involved in supporting a gift card service. Technology requirements were added to the design.

Also, since Mark was becoming familiar with the concepts of IT Service Management, he determined that he would need to address any of the Service Management tools and technology to see if any modifications needed to be made to support this new service.

Some of the Service Management tools and technology that he identified right away included the Service Portfolio, Service Catalog, Configuration Management System, Service Desk tools, and the Service Knowledge Management System. However, he knew that there would be other tools that would need to be considered through the design of this new service.

Together, Emil and Mark created the beginnings of a design document that addressed the service as a holistic service, instead of only as a new technology. Since starting to employ Service Management concepts, Mark discovered that the traditional view of IT is very short sighted and all aspects of a service must be considered when designing a new or changed service. Mark discovered that all aspect of this new service could not be provided by IT only, but IT and the business could provide all aspects of this service by working more closely together to meet the business desired outcomes.

PURPOSE

The purpose of Service Design is the design of new or changed services for introduction into the live environment to ensure consistency and integration within all activities and processes across the entire IT technology, providing end-to-end business-related functionality and quality. This means that Service Design must take a holistic approach to design that includes designing:

Management System and Tools

The tools and techniques required to manage the service

Standard Architectures

Ensuring that the design of the service is consistent with existing services and architectures

Technologies

The solution itself and its supporting technologies

Service Management Metrics

Measurements and metrics to ensure that the service meets its requirements and is being properly managed

Processes

Processes required to operate this service

The Goals of Service Design include:

Designing services to satisfy business objectives based on quality, compliance, risk and security requirements

Improving effectiveness and efficiency

Designing services that can be easily and efficiently developed and enhanced within appropriate timescales and costs, and reduce the long-term costs of service provision

Designing efficient and effective processes for the design, transition, operation and improvement of high quality IT services

Includes supporting tools, systems and information

Identify and manage risks before services go live

Assists in the development of policies and standards

Meet the current and identified future needs of the business through designing secure and resilient services

Develop skills and capability within IT

Move strategy and design activities into operational tasks

Contribute to the overall improvement of IT service quality

VALUE TO BUSINESS

Good design ensures that the service meets its business desired outcomes while conforming to the requirements and constraints of Service Strategy. It is important that the service is designed based on these business needs, and continual verification that the service that meets these needs is performed.

The value to business of Service Design includes:

> Reduced Total Cost of Ownership (TCO)
> Improved quality of service
> Improved consistency of service
> Improved implementation of new or changed services
> Alignment of services to the business
> Improved service performance
> Improved IT Governance
> Effective Service Management and ITSM processes
> Improved decision making based on higher quality information

KEY CONCEPTS

Service Design requires inputs from Service Strategy. These inputs include the Service Portfolio, where requirements are gathered and recorded and the strategies and constraints that services must meet.

The resulting solution from Service Design is more than just the technology but also the Service Management system and tools, standard architectures, processes and measurements and metrics. All of these parts of the solution support the transition, operation and improvement of the service.

These design components are documented in a Service Design Package (SDP) used by Service Transition to develop the service and transition it into operation.

All developers, project managers, and others who design services know that good design is invaluable to the business. Good design anticipates and resolves issues that often arise in the development stage or later. However, design is always the first thing to be eliminated when the pressures of time start to impact a service.

The Value of Design includes the following:

Agreed service levels ensuring critical business processes have the proper

focus

Understanding which business processes are critical and designing services to support those critical business processes

Measuring IT quality in business or user terms that are better understood

Understanding the business desired outcomes and designing measurements and metrics that map to these business desired outcomes, thus improving the communication with the business and increasing the perception of value

Mapping business processes to the IT infrastructure

Understanding how the IT technology supports the business processes and relating them to those business processes

Measuring services in relation to business processes

Providing the ability to measure how services meet the needs of the business processes

Mapping infrastructure resources to services

Understanding and mapping technology to services and storing this information in the Configuration Management System (CMS). We will explore the CMS later.

Providing end-to-end performance monitoring

Understanding the elements of the service that impact performance and being able to measure them throughout the entire service. This helps us to understand the end-user's perception of the performance of a service rather than just the IT perception of the service.

Good and proper design results in a solution that satisfies the business requirements, is easier to operate and support, and lowers the total cost of ownership (TCO) of the service. A properly designed service that includes all components of the service is far easier to transition and operate than a poorly designed service or one that does not include all of the necessary components.

Service Design ensures

> Services are business and customer oriented, focused and driven
>
> Services are cost effective and secure
>
> Services are flexible and adaptable, yet fit for purpose at the point of delivery
>
> Services can absorb an ever-increasing demand in the volume and speed of change
>
> Services meet increasing business demands for continuous operation
>
> Services are managed and operated to an acceptable level of risk
>
> Services are responsive, with appropriate availability matched to business needs

A service consists of far more than just the technology. A service requires people, processes, products (technology) and partners. These are the 4 P's of Service Design. This was discussed earlier.

For the exam, remember the 4 P's of Service Design; People, Products, Processes and Partners. This is highly likely to be on the exam.

Part of the design of a service includes understanding how the activities in the transition and operation stages of the Service Lifecycle will be sourced. Proper design considers these sourcing options to come up with the best option based on many things such as organizational abilities, culture, available resources, etc.

SOURCING OPTIONS

Obtaining services from an internal IT organization is not the only option that an organization has. In fact, many services that an organization uses are provided by outsourcers or vendors. This has the benefit of allowing the business to focus on the things that it does well without having to be concerned with activities that can be provided more effectively by other means.

Sourcing options include:

In-Sourcing

Performing all activities from within the organization

Outsourcing

Defining activities that are provided from outside the organization

Co-Sourcing

Combining the in-sourcing and outsourcing options to provide service

Partnership/Co-sourcing

Formal arrangements that leverage critical expertise of market opportunities

Business Process Outsourcing

Outsourcing of an entire business process

This is a popular option for many small to medium sized organizations that do not want to maintain their own Human Resources department, Payroll department, etc.

Application Service Provisioning (ASP)

Outsourcing access to critical and expensive applications

Reduces cost by paying for only a part of the application and its management

Knowledge Process Outsourcing (KPO)

Outsourcing of domain-based expertise

KPO is the newest form of outsourcing

Five Aspects of Design

Considering the five aspects of design when designing a service helps to ensure that the entire service can be implemented, transitioned, and operated efficiently and effectively. These five aspects include:

- The Service Solution itself, including resources and capabilities

- The Service Management systems and tools

- Technology and architectures to manage the technology

- Processes to transition, operate, and improve the service

- Measurement systems to design, transition, operate and improve the service, including measurements and metrics for the service, for the architecture and for the processes.

These five aspects of design are documented in the Service Package (SDP) that is output from Service Design.

Service Knowledge Management System (SKMS)

Within Service Design is the concept of the Service Knowledge Management Systems (SKMS). All information regarding a service is stored in the SKMS. Service Design is responsible for the design of the SKMS and the information that populates it. The SKMS is not limited to Service Design, however, and is used by the other Service Life-cycle stages.

The Service Knowledge Management System includes:

Service Scripts

Scripts used in diagnosing issues with the service at the Service Desk

Service Designs

The overall design of the service is stored and shared and will be helpful to other processes in evaluating the service and finding errors

Problems

Problems with the service are stored in the SKMS to be shared with others

Other information

Other information to support the service that is shared

SERVICE PORTFOLIO

Also included in the SKMS and of particular notice is the Service Portfolio. The Service Portfolio contains the list of all services for which commitments to the service have been made. The Service Portfolio maps business requirements to individual services to be used in the design stage. The Service Portfolio also includes the Service Pipeline, Service Catalog and Retired Services.

Service Pipeline

The Service Pipeline contains all services that have been conceived, are being evaluated or are being designed and developed. The Service Pipeline consists of all services that are not yet operational.

Service Catalog

The Service Catalog is a catalog of services that are available to the users of IT services. The Service Catalog lists all services that are operational.

Retired Services

Retired Services are all services that have been removed from service. The information regarding the service is retained as it may be referred to in the future.

The Service Portfolio is managed by the Service Portfolio Management process and will be presented in the Service Strategy processes section. The Service Catalog is managed by the Service Catalog Management process and will be presented in the Service Design processes section. The SKMS is managed by Knowledge Management and will be presented in the Service Transition processes section.

SERVICE LIFECYCLE STATUS

The Service Portfolio documents all services under consideration, being designed, in operation, and retired. The services within the Service Portfolio have a lifecycle within the Service Portfolio. The service lifecycle status determines whether they are in the Service Pipeline, the Service Catalog, or Retired Services.

There is overlap between services and which stage they are in, depending on the status. That is due to the fact that services are not just "thrown over the wall" when they pass from one stage to the next. The overlap is intended to make sure the service is passed to the next stage in a way that ensures acceptance of that service.

CHAPTER REVIEW

Definitions

Service Portfolio	Contains the list of all services for which commitments to the service have been made
Service Pipeline	Contains all services that have been conceived, are being evaluated or are being designed and developed.
Service Catalog	A catalog of services that are available to the users of IT services
Retired Services	All services that have been removed from service

Sourcing Options

In-Sourcing

Outsourcing

Co-Sourcing

Partnership/Co-sourcing

Business Process Outsourcing

Application Service Provisioning (ASP)

Knowledge Process Outsourcing (KPO)

Five Aspects of Design

The Service Solution itself, including resources and capabilities

The Service Management systems and tools

Technology and architectures to manage the technology

Processes to transition, operate, and improve the service

Measurement systems to design, transition, operate and improve the service, including measurements and metrics for the service, for the architecture and for the processes.

Service Design

Purpose

Provide guidance for the design of new or changed services for intro-duction into the live environment to ensure consistency and integration within all activities and processes across the entire IT technology, provid-ing end-to-end business-related functionality and quality.

Major Output
Service Design Package (SDP)

CHAPTER QUIZ

1.   The major output of Service Design is the _____.

     a.   Service Level Package

     b.   Service Operations Package

     c.   Technical Solutions

     d.   Service Design Package

2.   What is the newest form of outsourcing?

     a.   Application Service Provisioning

     b.   Partnership

     c.   Co-Sourcing

     d.   Business Process Outsourcing

     e.   Knowledge Process Outsourcing

3.   Match the following sourcing options with their descriptions.

     a.   Business Process Outsourcing

     b.   Insourcing

     c.   Knowledge Process Outsourcing

     d.   Application Service Provisioning

     e.   Outsourcing

     i.   External organizations perform the defined activities

     ii.   Outsourcing of applications

     iii.   Outsourcing of domain based expertise

     iv.   Internal organizations perform all activities

     v.   Outsourcing business processes

4.   What are the five aspects of Service Design?

   a.   Application and Software Engineering

   b.   Service Management Systems

   c.   Measurement Systems

   d.   Application Development

   e.   Quality Controls

   f.   Service Solutions

   g.   Technology and Management Architectures

   h.   Processes

5.   The Service Knowledge Management System (SKMS) contains the _____, which has the _____ as part of it.

   a.   Service Catalog & Service Requirements

   b.   Service Portfolio & Service Desk

   c.   Service Portfolio & Service Catalog

   d.   Service Requirements & Service Portfolio

6.   The _____ includes all services that are under consideration until they are released into operations.

   a.   Service Quality Plan

   b.   Service Portfolio

   c.   Service Catalog

   d.   Service Pipeline

9. Which of the following documents contains the subset of services visible to customers?

    a. Service Catalog
    b. Service Quality Plan
    c. Service Pipeline
    d. Service Portfolio

Answers

1. D
2. A, B, E, F, G
3. D
4. E
5. A – v, B – iv, C – iii, D – ii, E – ii
6. B, C, F, G, H
7. C
8. D
9. A

SERVICE TRANSITION OVERVIEW

OVERVIEW

The Service Transition stage of the Service Lifecycle takes as input the Service Design Package (SDP) from Service Design to build and prepare the service for operation in the live environment. Service Transition is responsible for managing the changes and releases to a service, as well as controlling modifications to a service.

In this chapter, the overview of Service Transition is discussed, including the purpose, objectives and value to business. Other key concepts, including the Service V Model, are also included.

Service Transition accepts the Service Design Package (SDP) from Service Design to ensure that all aspects of a service, not just the service technical solution, are transitioned into operation. This ensures that the service can be properly supported. The output of Service Transition is the Service Transition Package (STP) that includes the service, metrics and measurements, service levels, procedures, processes and knowledge of the service. The STP serves to ensure that the service can be properly supported in Service Operation, that it can be measured to ensure that it meets the needs of the business, and can be continually improved.

TRANSITIONING THE GIFT CARD SERVICE

Mark Renner recognizes through his study of the concepts of IT Service Management that transitioning a service into operation is where the highest risk is for a new service. The transition activities of a new or changed service can cause a great deal of interruption to the existing services and processes that support a service. To minimize the transition of the gift card service into operation, Mark established transition processes based on ITIL®.

These processes that Mark established are to minimize the risk of disruption to the business. They also ensure that expectations are well-established for both IT and the business so that everyone knows what to expect with this new service. Mark also ensured that one of the most commonly overlooked issues with new services, Early Life Support, is considered and the resources are allocated to support the service when it released to operation until the operations staff can fully support it.

To minimize disruption during the transition, Mark established a well-defined test and evaluation plan. This test and evaluation plan goes far beyond just testing the functionality of the IT portion of the service, but also includes all other aspects of the service. These aspects include ensuring that staff is trained in the new service and the support of the service, the roles and responsibilities to transition and support the service are well defined and considered early in the transition, the operational aspects of the service are tested and that the knowledge gained during the design and transition of the service is conveyed to the operations staff through the Service Knowledge Management System.

PURPOSE

Service Transition's main purpose is to manage the transition for a new service, or a change to a service, into production. This is done primarily through the processes of Change Management and Release and Deployment Management and controlled through the process of Service Asset and Configuration Management.

The other purposes of Service Transition include:

Planning and managing the build, test and deployment of a release into production

Providing a consistent and rigorous framework for transition

Establishing and maintaining the integrity of all identified service assets and their configurations

Providing knowledge and information regarding the service

Providing efficient repeatable build and installation mechanisms

Ensuring that the service can be managed, operated and supported

BUSINESS VALUE

Business obtains value from Service Transition through the assurance that the service is well-built and can be supported. Business also depends on Service Transition to align the new or changed service with the customer's business requirements and operations. Most of the time, a change to a service, including seemingly minor changes, are part of some larger business transition. The business must understand what the change to the service involves in order to prepare their business transition around this change.

Proper Service Transition also ensures that customers and users can use the new or changed service in a way that maximizes value to business operations. Service Transition includes aspects to communicate the change to the service to business and its users so that maximum value can be attained from the service.

Business benefits from Service Transition through this holistic approach to change and the ability to control change. With proper Service Transition processes, the business objectives can be more readily met in a predictable manner reducing the need for re-work and wasted time due to poor transition into operation.

Other benefits include:

> The ability to adapt quickly to new requirements and market developments

> Transition management of mergers, de-mergers, acquisitions and transfer of services

> The success rate of changes and releases for the business

> Improve predictions of service levels and warranties for new and changed services

> Improve confidence in the degree of compliance with business and governance requirements during change

> Reduce variation of actual against estimated with regard to approved resource plans and budgets

> Improve productivity of business and customer staff because of better planning and use of new and changed services

> Timely cancellation of changes to maintenance contracts for hardware

and software components are disposed or decommissioned

Improved understanding of the level of risk during and after change

GOALS AND OBJECTIVES

Service Transition ensures the integrity of a service during the transition to Service Operation. Service Transition also works closely with Continual Service Improvement as it is the Service Transition stage where improvements are realized.

Goals of Service Transition

> Set customer expectations on how the performance and use of the new or changed service can be used to enable business change

> Enable the business change project or customer to integrate a release into their business processes and services

> Reduce variations in the predicted and actual performance of the transitioned services

> Reduce the known errors and minimize the risks from transitioning the new or changed services into production

> Ensure that the service can be used in accordance with the requirements and constraints specified within the service requirements

Objectives of Service Transition

> Plan and manage the resources to establish a new or changed service into production within the predicted cost, quality and time estimates

> Ensure there is minimal unpredictable impact on the production services, operations and support organization

> Increase the customer, user and Service Management staff satisfaction with the Service Transition practices, including deployment of the new or changed service, communications, release documentation, training and knowledge transfer

> Increase proper use of the services, underlying applications and technology solutions

> Provide clear and comprehensive plans that enable the customer and

business change projects to align their activities with the Service Transition plans

Key Concepts

Service Transition is a critical stage between Service Design and Service Operation. Far too often, IT organizations deploy services into production by "tossing them over the fence." This results in a poorly deployed service that fails to meet business objectives during a painful deployment process.

Lately, the news has contained many articles specifically targeting the transportation industry. These articles have reported numerous transportation disruptions. The primary cause of these disruptions has been poorly transitioned services. One airline in particular experienced long ticketing delays due to improperly released applications that support their services.

In order to overcome these difficulties, Service Transition processes formalize the transition of a service, or a change to a service, into operation. Service Transition does not end when the service is "operational," but includes support through the service's early life to ensure that the business objectives can be met and the service is well supported. This overlap between Service Transition and Service Operation is called Early Life Support.

Service V Model

The Service V Model is an important concept in Service Transition. The Service V Model shows that for any business requirement, there must be equivalent validation and testing of that requirement to ensure its utility and warranty.

On the left side, the Service V Model starts with the business requirements and decomposes these requirements into more specific specifications until a solution has been reached and developed. This solution is then assembled and tested against the levels of specification until it is finally validated against the business requirements.

The Service V Model ensures not only the proper levels of testing but also that the Service Package has been validated and supported by the appropriate service offerings, supporting agreements, and supporting contracts.

Service V Model

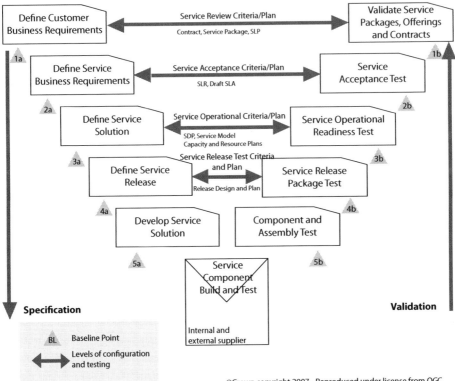

Figure 8 - Service V Model

Based on the business requirements, specifications are developed. These specifications, when developed, become baselined and are under the control of Change Management. When assemblies and releases are developed, they are also under the control of Change Management. This ensures that the specifications and the resulting validated outputs are controlled.

Definitive Media Library

The Definitive Media Library (DML) is a repository for all media in its definitive state. The media assets of an organization traditionally include software. However, in today's environment, other types of media are becoming quite prevalent. These types of media may include banners for web pages, video clips, movies, flash components and many other

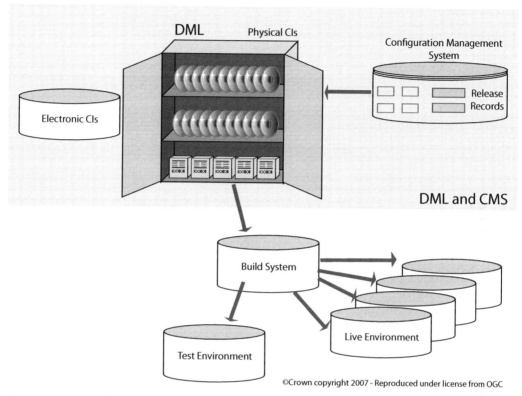

Figure 9 - Service Transition and the Definitive Media Library

forms of media that are required for a service.

Before software and any media is installed into the production environment, it must first be checked into the DML as an authorized version of that media. The DML has required check-in procedures to ensure that the media is approved, virus free, definitive, and properly prepared for use in the operational environment. The check-in procedures of the media also ensure that the media is of the correct quality to be included as part of a service.

These procedures also ensure that services can be properly built, provide better control, promote standardization in the environment, and ensure that only authorized components are in use in the live environment. A service must be built on components of known quality. The DML assists in controlling these assets to ensure that only authorized, quality components are used.

This check-in to the DML is applied to both developed software and purchased software.

Any software in the DML is in its definitive, installable state, rather than source code. Source code control is the development team's responsibility and development should turn over fully completed, installable software, including the installation packages. However, there is an exception. While source code control is primarily the responsibility of development, some source code is included as part of a service. Some examples of source code as part of the definitive version of a service include Java script, PHP source, etc.

The Definitive Media Library is defined as *one or more locations in which the definitive and approved versions of all software Configuration Items are securely stored*. The DML may also contain associated components such as licenses and documentation regarding the media. The media in the DML is under the control of Change and Release Management and is recorded in the Configuration Management System. The DML may be multiple locations depending on the organization.

When a new release is being prepared, only media contained within the DML are to be used as part of the release. This ensures that the media components of that release are of sufficient quality.

The DML must be kept separate from development, test and live environments. This prevents contamination of the media in the DML in the event any other environments were to become corrupted.

Definitive Spares (DS)

Definitive Spares involve providing secure storage areas of definitive hardware spares. These definitive storage areas maintain spare hardware components and assemblies, which are maintained at the same level as comparative systems in the live environment.

The DS ensures ease of implementation when new hardware is required or when components fail and require replacement. All hardware in the DS should be pre-configured to organizational standards to reduce the time it takes to provision this hardware. Implementing a DS helps to ensure standard hardware configurations are used throughout the organization where possible.

CHAPTER REVIEW

Service Transition

Purpose

Provide guidance to manage the transition for a new service or a change to a service into production

Business Value

Assurance that the service is well built and can be supported

Major Output

Service Transition Package

Service V Model

Represents levels of validation and testing for a new or changed service

Definitive Media Library (DML)

Repository for all media in its definitive state

Definitive Spares (DS)

Secure storage areas of definitive hardware spares

CHAPTER QUIZ

1.   The major input to Service Transition includes:

    a.   Service Transition Package
    b.   Service Design Package
    c.   Service Quality Plan
    d.   Service Level Package

2.   The major output of Service Transition includes:

    a.   Service Quality Plan
    b.   Service Transition Package
    c.   Service Level Package
    d.   Service Design Package

3.   The Service Transition Package is output to what Service Lifecycle stage?

    a.   Service Design
    b.   Service Operation
    c.   Continual Service Improvement
    d.   Service Strategy

4.   One of the values to business of Service Transition is to align the new or changed service with the customer's business requirements and business operations. The other is:

    a.   Ensure that customers and users can use the new or changed service in a way that maximizes value to the business operations
    b.   Provide the highest quality service at the lowest cost
    c.   Ensure that Service Operation understands all aspects of the service when it is released
    d.   Ensure that services can be transitioned as effectively as possible

5. The model that builds in service validation and testing early in the service life-cycle is called what?

    a. Quality Assurance Plan
    b. Service Testing and Validation
    c. The Service V Model
    d. The Service T Model

Answers

1. B
2. B
3. B
4. A
5. C

8

SERVICE OPERATION OVERVIEW

OVERVIEW

Service Operation is where the value is delivered to the customer and the strategy of the organization is executed. Think about an automobile manufacturer; the manufacturer develops a strategy for the market, designs an automobile to meet customer requirements, builds the car, and delivers it for sale through an automobile dealership. Up to this point, there has been a lot of work put into the manufacture of that car, but it isn't until the car is sold and the new owner drives the car off the lot that the value of the vehicle is realized.

Service Operation delivers this value by supporting the solutions that the customer requires. Service Operation does this through assuring the service is well supported and available to the customer.

This chapter introduces the basic concepts of Service Operation including its purpose, objectives and value to business. Service Operation constantly has to balance opposing forces. These forces and considerations will also be explored.

PURPOSE

The purpose of Service Operation is to coordinate and carry out the activities and processes required to deliver and manage services at agreed levels to business users and customers. The objective of Service Operation is the responsibility for the ongoing management of the technology that is used to deliver and support services.

Service Operation receives the Service Transition Package as input, which includes the service solution, architectures, processes, Service Management tools and methods for metrics and measurement. Service Operation uses the Service Transition Package to ensure that the service is well supported. The main output of Service Operation is value to the customers and the Service Operation reports to Continual Service Improvement.

KEY CONCEPTS

Value to the business is realized through Service Operation. However, Service Operation has some specific challenges. Once the service is delivered, it is Service Operation's responsibility. Many times the scoping and funding of the service fails to include the operational costs of the service, only the design, development, and rollout of the service. Service Operation is then forced to support a service without the appropriate funding. This is exacerbated when the service has flaws in it and there is no funding to address these flaws.

Once a service has been introduced to the customer and users, the service is taken for granted. It is assumed that the new service is part of the standard within IT even though the financial and support aspects have not been considered. Service Design and Service Transition attempt to remedy this issue by insuring that all aspects of a service are considered so that it can be supported effectively and efficiently as a continuing concern in Service Operation.

SERVICE OPERATION BALANCE

Service Operation is constantly striving to balance the continuous demands IT faces. Changes in business, changes in technology and legislative changes produce conflict in IT. Service Operation's challenge is to provide standard levels of service despite these conflicts.

Internal View vs. External View

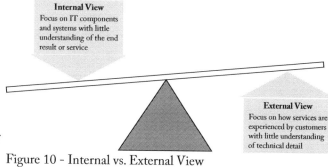

One area of balance to be achieved is an internal versus external view of IT. Internal views of IT focus on the components, technology and systems that are used to deliver service. IT with an internal view usually consists of "silos" or multiple departments that focus on their individual areas without a view of the overall service. Organizations that are too internally focused fail to understand the service being provided and risk the danger of failing to meet business requirements.

Figure 10 - Internal vs. External View

An organization with an extreme external view focuses on the end-result to the business with little understanding or concern about the technical detail of the service. An organization that is too externally focused tends to under-deliver on the promises made to the business.

Both views must be balanced in order to achieve the desired business outcomes while still being able to support the technology that provides the service.

Stability vs. Responsiveness

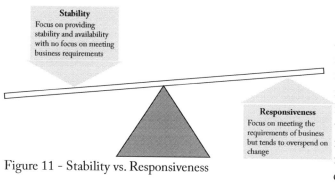

Figure 11 - Stability vs. Responsiveness

Another challenge that IT faces is to provide a stable environment for the business while still responding to changing business needs. IT organizations that are too responsive excel in meeting the needs of the business, but tend to overspend on changes. Organizations that are too focused on stability provide a status quo for the business, but fail to meet business requirements and their changing needs.

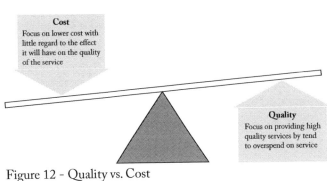

Figure 12 - Quality vs. Cost

Quality vs. Cost

Quality versus cost is another common conflict. While business demands high quality, this quality comes at a higher cost as the quality requirements rise. The cost of quality is not directly proportional to the quality required. The majority of quality can be provided at a lower cost, but as incremental improvements in quality are required, the added costs increase.

Organizations that are too quality-focused provide great service, but tend to overspend on the costs of those services. Organizations that are too cost focused are in danger of losing quality because of cost cutting. However, IT constantly struggles with the demand to improve quality while still cutting costs.

Reactive vs. Proactive

IT organizations must also balance being reactive versus being proactive. Reactive organizations do not act until they are triggered to perform some action. Over time, all work is reactive with little opportunity to be proactive. The more reactive an IT organization becomes, the less likely they are able to effectively support the business strategy.

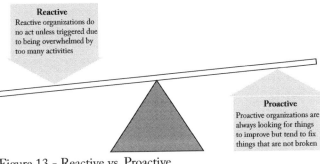

Figure 13 - Reactive vs. Proactive

Proactive organizations are always looking for ways to improve their services. When IT organizations are too proactive, services that are not broken are trying to be fixed or improved. This results in services being overly expensive.

CHAPTER REVIEW

Service Operation

Purpose

Coordinate and carry out the activities and processes required to deliver and manage services at agreed levels to business users and customers.

Service Operation Balance

Internal vs. External

Stability vs. Responsiveness

Quality vs. Cost

Reactive vs. Proactive

CHAPTER QUIZ

1.   The major input to Service Operation is what?

        a.   Service Level Package
        b.   Service Transition Package
        c.   Service Portfolio
        d.   Service Design Package
        e.   Service Catalog

2.   The objective of the Service Operations stage of the Service Lifecycle is:

        a.   Provide services at the lowest cost
        b.   Ensures availability of services
        c.   Ongoing management of the technology that is used to deliver and support services
        d.   Ensure that services meet their defined service levels

3.   The output of Service Operation is what?

        a.   Services
        b.   Value
        c.   Quality
        d.   Availability

4.   Match these conflicting operational requirements that demand balance.

    a.   Internal View

    b.   Stability

    c.   Quality

    d.   Reactive

    i.   Cost

    ii.   Proactive

    iii.   Responsiveness

    iv.   External View

Answers

1.   B
2.   C
3.   B
4.   A – iv, B – iii, C – i, D – ii

9

CONTINUAL SERVICE IMPROVEMENT OVERVIEW

OVERVIEW

The Continual Service Improvement (CSI) stage of the Service Lifecycle focuses on ensuring that services, and all elements that make up the service, are aligned and continually realigned to ensure it meets business needs and can be improved. Drawing an analogy to a popular television show, CSI is aptly named because it focuses on the forensics of the service to insure that it is properly measured. There is nothing out of scope for CSI as it strives to provide measurements not only for the service itself, but also the processes that support it; the design processes, the transition processes, the strategy and the organization.

In this chapter, you will be introduced to Continual Service Improvement, its key concepts, overall activities, purpose, objectives, scope and value to business.

PURPOSE

CSI ensures that a services is continually aligned and realigned to the needs of the business. There is little that is out of scope for CSI in that anything that can be improved is a candidate for CSI. However, Continual Service Improvement focuses on three key areas; the overall health of IT Service Management as a formal discipline, ensuring that services are constantly aligned with the Service Portfolio, and the maturing of the enabling IT processes for each stage in the Service Lifecycle.

VALUE TO BUSINESS

The value of CSI is obvious, but commonly overlooked. CSI strives to improve quality of services, Return on Investment (ROI) and Value of Investment (VOI). ROI is improved by identifying opportunities to lower costs. VOI is improved by identifying opportunities to provide increased value for the cost. VOI includes the intangible benefits including:

> Increased organizational competency
>
> Improved integration between people and processes
>
> Reduced redundancy increasing business throughput
>
> Minimized lost opportunities
>
> Assured regulatory compliance that will minimize costs and reduce risk
>
> Improved ability to rapidly react to change

Improvements are defined as *outcomes that when compared to the before state, show a measurable increase in a desirable metric or decrease in an undesirable metric.*

Benefits are defined as *achievements through realization of improvements usually, but not always, expressed in monetary terms.*

Return on Investment (ROI) is defined as *the difference between the benefit achieved and the amount expended to achieve that benefit expressed as a percentage.*

Value of Investment (VOI) is defined as *the extra value created by establishment of the benefits that include non-monetary or long-term outcomes*

PDCA/DEMING CYCLE

CSI is based on the principles of continuous quality control first published by Edwards Deming in the 1940's. In the 1940's, Mr. Deming developed his philosophy of improvement through his 14 points of attention to managers. Mr. Deming developed a process led approach that underpins the concepts within Continual Service Improvement.

Mr. Deming's Plan-Do-Check-Act cycle is a continuous process to identify opportunities for improvement. Taken as basic common sense today, the Plan-Do-Check-Act cycle was a novel approach to manufacturing in the 1940's. It essentially says that you should plan what you are going to do, do what was planned, check to see if you obtained the desired outcome according to the plan, and, act to improve the plan before you act again. Each iteration of this cycle will improve the base level of quality.

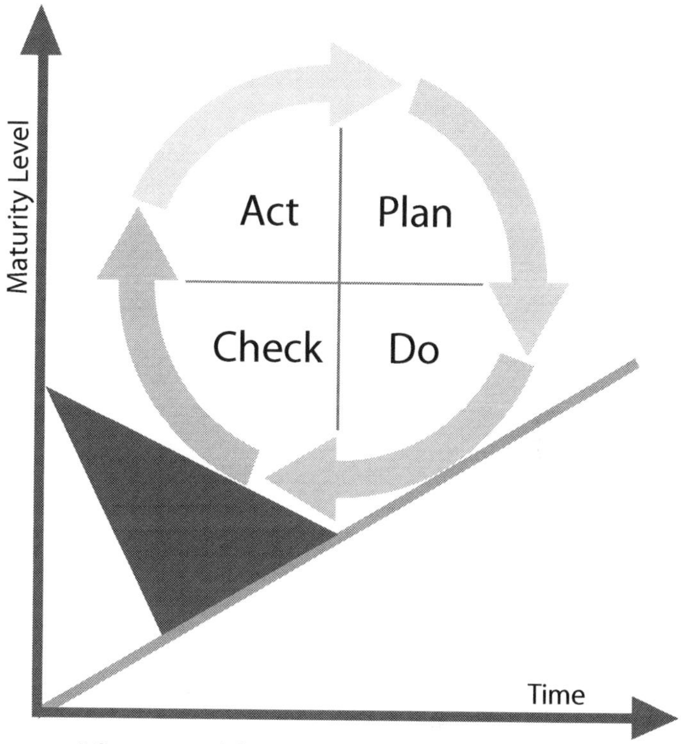

©Crown copyright 2007 - Reproduced under license from OGC

Figure 14 - Plan-Do-Check-Act Cycle

Deming's improvement cycle is the basis for most, if not all, quality standards in existence today such as 6-Sigma, TQM and others.

Overall CSI Activities

The activities around CSI are focused on the continued audit of services, processes, procedures and organization to identify opportunities for improvement. All other Service Lifecycle stages provide input into the activities in CSI. CSI's activities include:

Reviewing management information and trends

Periodically conducting maturity assessments to identify areas of improvement

Periodically conducting internal audits to verify process compliance

Reviewing existing deliverables for relevance to ensure deliverables are still needed

Making improvement recommendations for approval

Conducting customer satisfaction surveys

Conducting external and internal service reviews to identify opportunities for improvement

All of these activities must be planned and are not automatic. Many of these activities take place in other Service Lifecycle stage processes.

CSI Model

The CSI approach identifies six questions that have associated actions to determine the answers. This approach helps to ensure that improvements are objective, measurable, and meet the business strategy.

What is the vision?

The "What is the vision?" question is answered by identifying the business vision, mission, goals, and objectives that need to be addressed.

Where are we now?

The "Where are we now?" question is answered through performing baseline assessments that obtain an accurate, unbiased snapshot of where the organization is. These assessments measure the organization in a objective manner to provide a basis for comparison later.

Where do we want to be?

The "Where do we want to be?" question is answered through identification of measurable targets that detail the CSI plan to achieve higher quality service provision. These measurable targets should be objective

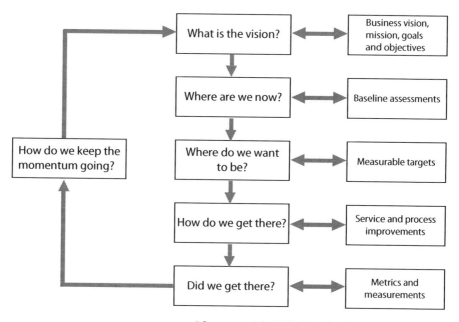

Figure 15 - CSI Model

and readily accepted by everyone. While it is easy to identify a measurable target, it should be an objective target to ensure that the target achieves the desired objective and accurately reflects the desired state.

How do we get there?

The "How do we get there?" question is answered through our service and process improvements developed based on the principles defined in the vision. This is where the process improvement or re-engineering work takes place.

Did we get there?

The "Did we get there?" question is answered through metrics and measurements that ensure milestones were achieved, process compliance is high, and business objectives and priorities are met. This is where measurements are compared against our baseline that was established through the "Where are we now?" question.

How do we keep the momentum going?

The "How do we keep the momentum going?" question ensures that the improvements made are established and become part of the organization. Based on these improvements, the organization can establish new baselines for continued improvement.

MEASUREMENT

Service Measurement measures the services and processes to identify opportunities for continual improvement. When measuring, the following questions need to be answered regarding these measurements:

Why are we monitoring and measuring?

This question ensures that we know the reason for the monitoring and measuring, and our efforts are aligned to those reasons. Many IT organizations measure things without understanding the reason for the measurement only to become overwhelmed with data.

When do we stop?

This question acknowledges that measurements should not go on forever and that the effort expended to collect the measurements are valued.

Is anyone using the data?

This question ensures that the data is actually being used. It is quite common for organizations to begin collecting metrics and creating reports only to deliver these reports to no one. This question must be asked periodically to ensure that more work is not created which does not add value.

Do we still need this?

Periodically, this question should be asked to ensure that metrics are being collected only for the things that are needed and extra effort is not being expended which does not add value.

There are four reasons for Service Measurement. These reasons are:

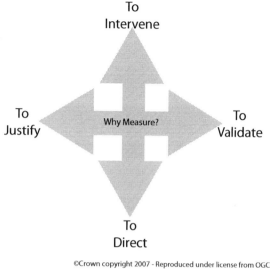

©Crown copyright 2007 - Reproduced under license from OGC

Figure 16 - Reasons to Measure

To validate

Measurements validate that previous decisions and actions were the correct decisions and actions.

To direct

Measurements provide data that is used to make decisions and provide direction

To justify

Measurements provide proof that justify particular actions

To intervene

Measurements are used to intervene and provide changes in direction

Baselines

A baseline is a metric measured at a particular point in time in order to compare a later measured metric. A baseline comparison can assist in determining if the process is improving or show general direction of trends. Baselines are the important starting point for later comparison. Therefore, in order to be recognized and accepted throughout the organization, baselines must be objective, documented and agreed upon.

The CSI approach uses assessments to determine where an organization is at a certain point in time. These assessments document baselines that are referred to later as a point of comparison to see if the desired improvements have been made.

TYPES OF METRICS

There are three basic types of metrics that can be collected and used by CSI. Technology metrics are most common and are often collected today. Technology metrics are associated with the actual components and applications that make up a service.

Process metrics are intended to measure the performance of a process in an effort to improve process efficiency and effectiveness. These metrics take the form of Critical Success Factors (CSF's), Key Performance Indicators (KPI's) and activity metrics within the process.

Service metrics measure the overall ability of a service to achieve its goal. These metrics measure end-to-end performance and often include individual technology metrics that correlate with each other to provide a view into the overall service performance.

Chapter Review

Definitions

Improvements	Outcomes that, when compared to the before state, show a measurable increase in a desirable metric or decrease in an undesirable metric
Benefits	Achievements through realization of improvements usually, but not always, expressed in monetary terms
Return on Investment (ROI)	The difference between the benefit achieved and the amount expended to achieve that benefit expressed as a percentage
Value of Investment (VOI)	The extra value created by establishment of the benefits that include non-monetary or long-term outcomes
Baseline	Metric measured at a particular point in time in order to compare a later measured metric

Continual Service Improvement

Purpose

Ensures that a service is continually aligned and realigned with the needs of the business

Deming's Plan-Do-Check-Act Cycle

A continuous process to identify opportunities for improvement

CSI Model

What is the vision?

Where are we now?

Where do we want to be?

How do we get there?

Did we get there?

How do we keep the momentum going?

Questions for Measuring

Why are we monitoring and measuring?

When do we stop?

Is anyone using the data?

Do we still need this?

Reasons for Service Measurement

To validate

To direct

To justify

To intervene

Types of metrics

Quantitative

Qualitative

CHAPTER QUIZ

1.   These are used to establish a basis for later comparison:

      a.   Baselines

      b.   Snapshots

      c.   Artifacts

      d.   Trend Analysis

2.   Arrange the questions related to the CSI approach in order.

      a.   Where do we want to be?

      b.   What is the vision?

      c.   How do we keep the momentum going?

      d.   How do we get there?

      e.   Where are we now?

      f.   Did we get there?

3.   What are the three types of metrics?

      a.   Process Metrics

      b.   Service Metrics

      c.   Technology Metrics

      d.   Component Metrics

4. The difference between the benefit achieved and the amount expended to achieve the benefit, expressed as a percentage, is called what?

    a. Improvement
    b. Value of Investment (VOI)
    c. Benefit
    d. Return on Investment (ROI)

5. Gains achieved through realization of improvements, usually, but not always, expressed in monetary terms is called what?

    a. Value of Investment (VOI)
    b. Benefit
    c. Return on Investment (ROI)
    d. Improvement

6. Outcomes that, when compared to the before state, show a measurable increase in a desirable metric or decrease in an undesirable metric is called what?

    a. Value of Investment (VOI)
    b. Benefit
    c. Return on Investment (ROI)
    d. Improvement

7. Activities for Continual Service Improvement come naturally and do not have to be deliberately planned in the Service Lifecycle.

    a. True
    b. False

8. Extra value created by establishment of benefits that include non-monetary or long-term outcomes is called what?

   a. Return on Investment (ROI)

   b. Improvement

   c. Benefit

   d. Value of Investment (VOI)

9. Validation is only one reason for measuring services. What are the other three?

   a. Intervention

   b. Justification

   c. Direction

   d. Promotions

   e. Improvement

10. What are the steps in order of the Deming Cycle?

    a. Plan, Check, Do, Act

    b. Plan, Do, Act, Check

    c. Plan, Do, Check, Act

    d. Plan, Act, Check, Do

11. What is the scope of Continual Service Improvement (pick 3)?

    a. Continual collection of requirements to improve services

    b. Maturity of the enabling IT processes for each service in the Service Lifecycle

    c. Overall health of ITSM as a discipline

    d. Continual alignment and realignment of the portfolio of IT services with the business needs

12.   The value to business of Continual Service Improvement includes what?

    a.   Lowering costs

    b.   Improving Value on Investment (VOI)

    c.   Improving service, quality and satisfaction

    d.   Improving Return on Investment (ROI)

    e.   All of the above

13.   One of the purposes of Continual Service Improvement is to continually align and realign IT services to meet changing business needs. What is the other?

    a.   Continually improve the quality of a service

    b.   Ensure metrics are collected to support continual improvement activities

    c.   Implement processes with defined goals, objectives and relevant measurements

    d.   Improve cost effectiveness

14.   Match the concept with the CSI approach question.

    a.   What is the vision?

    b.   Where are we now?

    c.   Where do we want to be?

    d.   How do we get there?

    e.   Did we get there?

    i.   Service and Process improvement

    ii.   Baseline assessments

    iii.   Measurable targets

    iv.   Mission, goals, objectives

    v.   Metrics and Measurements

Answers

1. A
2. B, E, A, D, F, C
3. A, B, C
4. D
5. B
6. D
7. B
8. D
9. A, B, C
10. C
11. B, C, D
12. E
13. C
14. A – iv, B – ii, C – iii, D – i, E - v

Service Strategy Shared Activities

Overview

The Service Strategy stage of the Service Lifecycle has shared activities that guide the overall direction of IT. These activities focus on identifying the market that IT is in, identifying IT's customers and developing a strategy for execution.

Geppetto Garcia's

Mark Renner, CIO of Geppetto Garcia's has recognized that he has two markets to serve. These markets include the internal corporate market and the restaurant market. Within the restaurant market, Mark identified three key services; Inventory Control service, Employee Time Scheduling service and the Ordering and Payment service.

These services have been identified and documented at a high level in the Service Portfolio. The Service Portfolio documents all services that the Service Provider has made any commitment to provide including any service that has been thought of, but not yet developed. The Service Portfolio records the business requirements of the service.

Mark and his Service Owners developed Service Assets for these identified services. These Service Assets include ensuring that the right components, people, organization and knowledge are in place to design, transition and support these services. One of the services, for example, is the Ordering and Payment service. This service requires hardware and software components to operate. It also requires network services within each restaurant, as well as a link back to the corporate office. To ensure that this service provides value, the service must be well supported. Mark would ensure that this service can be supported by training his staff on how to support it, develop processes to support it, and ensure that the knowledge of the service, including end-user training, is provided for this service.

ACTIVITIES

There are four major activities in Service Strategy that assist with development of the Service Level Package that serves as input to Service Design. These activities are defining the market, developing the offerings, developing strategic assets and preparing for execution.

DEFINE THE MARKET

This activity is focused on understanding who IT's customers are and identifying customer assets. This activity is critical in ensuring that the proper services are developed that meet the needs of the business.

Once the customer is identified, this activity continues by identifying the customer's assets. A customer's assets are those things that a customer values that enable them to achieve their business desired outcomes. For example, customer assets can include capital equipment, intellectual property or processes.

Defining the market starts with understanding the major market drivers. These market drivers provide an overview for the IT strategy.

There are two perspectives when defining a market strategy. The first is to develop a strategy for specific services, such as creating a strategy to capitalize on a specific capability in online services. Popular online shopping, auction and reservations businesses are good examples. These companies built strategies around their ability to develop web-based capabilities.

The second perspective is to develop services that align to the strategy. An organization may decide to enter a particular market for a particular customer segment. Services are then created to support that strategy. The emergence of online banking is an example. These companies, forced to respond to customer needs and demands, developed an online strategy, then developed their service assets to support this strategy.

Identifying customers is a top priority. Without understanding the customer, it is difficult to understand the market being served. In order to succeed in their business, customers either develop or purchase assets. Assets can be in the form of equipment, knowledge and business processes, among others. We must understand these assets in order to assist the business in capitalizing on their assets.

For example, a popular company that specializes in online auctioning relies on linking buyers and sellers so that they can conduct commerce. The company has recognized the importance of this "online community." This online community is one of their assets that distinguish them from their competitors. The company then decided to provide a mechanism for potential buyers to announce the items they want to buy, thus increasing the potential to link buyers and sellers. A service was developed to enable this mechanism to capitalize on this customer asset.

A customer's goal is to achieve their business desired outcomes. IT's goal is to provide services that facilitate achieving these business goals. Through analysis of these business desired outcomes, it can be determined which desired outcomes are served and which are not well-served. The desired outcomes that are not well-served become opportunities to explore for new or updated services.

Develop the Offerings

The develop the offerings activity documents the required service in the service portfolio ensuring that the service description is aligned with the customer's assets and business desired outcomes. This activity also identifies the capabilities and resources (service assets) that can be leveraged to provide this identified service.

The Service Portfolio represents commitments made to customers. The Service Portfolio documents all services, including the services being considered, developed, provided and retired. The Service Portfolio documents services in terms of business value and is supported by a business case. This ensures that the business desired outcomes are not overlooked or ignored.

Develop Strategic Assets

This activity focuses on developing the resources and capabilities to support the services that meet business requirements.

Beginning with a focus on customer assets, IT can develop its own strategic assets utilizing its capabilities and resources to develop services. Some customers may not entrust their strategic assets to a provider right away. It may require gaining trust over time by starting out with a small service to enable their business desired outcomes until the value has been shown and proven.

Prepare for Execution

Prepare for execution identifies the IT strategy based on both internal and external strategic assessments. This activity then defines the requirements and procedures for the remaining Service Lifecycle stages. These requirements and procedures are documented in the Service Level Package (SLP).

Preparing for service execution is a continual activity. When a service is first planned, the external and internal factors are assessed to establish the objectives. From these objectives, a strategy is generated that outlines the vision, policies, plans and actions required of that service. A major output of the strategy is to determine the requirements for the remaining stages, particularly around measurement and evaluation of the service. This major output is the Service Level Package in which these requirements are documented.

Strategic assessments strive to answer questions regarding our services. These questions include:

Which of our services or service varieties are the most distinctive?

What can customers not substitute?

Which of our services or service varieties are most profitable?

Include monetary, profit, social, health, or other major benefits depending on your business desired outcomes.

Which of our customers and stakeholders are the most satisfied?

Must understand first how customers determine satisfaction

Which customers, channels, or purchase occasions are the most profitable?

Where are we recovering the most money from our services?

Which of our activities in the value chain are most effective?

What are we doing right?

The answers to these questions reveal patterns regarding services.

Setting objectives involves identifying the actions required in order to realize a strategy. These actions should be well thought out and formulated in a way that focuses all activities toward the defined strategy. The key benefit to setting objectives is that ambiguity is removed from the organization's activities and aligned to the overall strategy.

The objectives and resulting actions should align IT's service assets (comprised of capabilities and resources) to the customer's business desired outcomes. Focusing on the business desired outcomes helps the IT organization set priorities for their limited resources, including focus, time, people and funding.

The defined service should include the elements that are required for success. These critical success factors (CSF's) assist in determining the underlying requirements for a service to help ensure the success of that service.

CSF's, combined with a competitive analysis identifies areas where the IT organization's services can be differentiated from other competitors. Performing this analysis readily identifies areas where further investment should be made and areas where the IT organization provides comparatively little differential value. If it costs more to provide the service ourselves when there are more effective alternatives, these alternatives should be considered allowing the organization to focus on the services that add differential value.

Every IT organization has limited resources. These resources are in the form of time, money, people, knowledge and capabilities. Investments in services must be prioritized to areas that have the highest impact on the customer's business in a balanced and cost-justifiable manner. To prioritize, the under-served customers must be identified to understand why the needs are not being properly met. To meet these needs usually involves greater performance or a more innovative approach to the service.

A SWOT analysis (Strengths, Weaknesses, Opportunities, Threats) is an analysis technique to identify which market spaces to expand and which should be avoided. Market spaces to avoid can be served by vendors or suppliers as needed. The SWOT analysis assists with decision making with regard to understanding market spaces, what services to offer, what customers to serve, the application of service models to existing or considered services, and the Service Catalog.

CHAPTER REVIEW

Service Strategy Shared Activities

> Define the market
> Develop the offerings
> Develop strategic assets
> Prepare for execution

Chapter Quiz

1.   The four Service Strategy shared activities are what?

    a.   Develop the Offerings
    b.   Service Portfolio Management
    c.   Prepare for Execution
    d.   Define the Market
    e.   Plan for Improvement
    f.   Develop Strategic Assets

2.   Match the activity with its objective.

    a.   Understand the customer
    b.   Identify capabilities and resources
    c.   Improve Service Management
    d.   Assess strategy and generate strategy

    i.   Prepare for Execution
    ii.   Define the Market
    iii.   Develop Strategic Assets
    iv.   Develop the Offerings

3.   The Service Portfolio:

    a.   Represents commitments made to provide services
    b.   Documents services being transitioned to operation
    c.   Includes the Service Catalog
    d.   Lists services that have been retired
    e.   All of the above

4.   Preparing for execution involves performing a strategic asset as well as generating a strategy. What are the four outputs when generating a strategy?

a.   Roadmap

b.   Vision

c.   Actions

d.   Plans

e.   Policies

Answers

1. A, C, D, F
2. A – ii, B – iv, C – iii, D – i
3. E
4. B, C, D, E

11

SERVICE STRATEGY PROCESSES

OVERVIEW

This chapter introduces the three Service Strategy processes; Service Portfolio Management, Demand Management, and Financial Management. These processes in particular overlap with other Service Lifecycle stages. While they are presented in Service Strategy and play an important part in development of the IT strategy, these processes should be kept in mind when learning the other Service Lifecycle stages.

Service Portfolio Management is responsible for making decisions regarding services and the allocation of service assets to those services. Demand Management analyzes the sources of demand for services to identify underlying patterns in an effort to anticipate or influence the demand. Financial Management is the process responsible to manage the funding of services and ensure the proper stewardship of funds.

These processes commonly share decision-making regarding services. Through these processes, decisions are made to determine which services are viable, which are not, and ensure that the services have the appropriate financial commitment.

SERVICE PORTFOLIO MANAGEMENT

GEPPETTO GARCIA'S

Mark Renner, CIO of Geppetto Garcia's, recognizes the need to create a portfolio of services. Mark understands that without having a consistent, documented portfolio of services, it is difficult to represent to the business what IT is providing or planning to provide to support the business' desired outcomes. If Mark cannot communicate the services and how they align to the desired outcomes of the business, it is difficult to communicate the value that IT provides, and even more difficult to justify funding for resources to support the business.

Mark's Service Portfolio documents all services that have been conceived, are in operation or have been retired. These services are documented in terms of the value that they provide to the business. Using the services defined in the Service Portfolio, Mark can better evaluate the relative importance of each service to ensure that the greatest focus of resources are directed to the services that provide the most value. This helps Mark control the risk within IT and the affects of that risk to the business.

OVERVIEW

Service Portfolio Management (SPM) is responsible for maximizing the return on investment while managing risk. Service Portfolio Management does this by describing services in terms of business value and articulating the provider's response to the needs of the business.

Service Portfolio Management is a dynamic method for governing investments in Service Management across the enterprise and managing them for value. The main tool in Service Portfolio Management is the Service Portfolio. The Service Portfolio assists this governance by documenting all services under consideration, being developed, being transitioned, operational or retired.

The Service Portfolio answers the following questions regarding service:

> Why should a customer buy these services?
>
> Why should they buy these services from us?
>
> What are the pricing or chargeback models?
>
> What are our strengths and weaknesses, priorities and risk?
>
> How should our resources and capabilities be allocated?

The Service Portfolio represents the complete set of services managed by the Service Provider. The Service Portfolio includes three catalogs; the Service Pipeline, Service Catalog and retired services. The Service Portfolio documents all services being considered, being designed, transitioning to operation, in operation, or retired from service.

The diagram below shows the Service Portfolio and its various components. The Service Portfolio draws on a common pool of resources (IT staff) to evaluate, design, transition, operate and continually improve services. The Service Portfolio assists in the prioritization of where these resources should focus to ensure that the highest priority services received the attention they require.

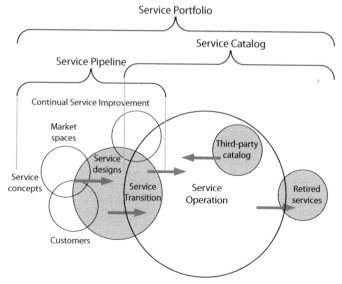

Figure 17 - Service Portfolio and its components

The Service Portfolio consists of the Service Pipeline, the Service Catalog, and retired services. The Service Pipeline is where requirements for services are collected to evaluate these requirements to determine if investment in a service is warranted and how resources should be allocated. The Service Pipeline draws upon the information collected in the Service Strategy shared activities about customers and market spaces.

The Service Catalog is a catalog of services that are available to customers and users of IT's services. The Service Catalog contains descriptions of all services that are operational, and should include any third party services that IT leverages. An example of this is mobile phones. IT itself does not supply the mobile phones, but relies on vendors for the phones. IT adds value to this service by supporting the phone, managing payments to the vendor, and vendor selection.

Retired services are those services that are no longer in operation. These services are documented in the Service Portfolio to retain the information for later use, if required. Once a service is retired, the information about that service may be useful if the service needs to be offered again, or a new service developed based on some of the characteristics of the retired service.

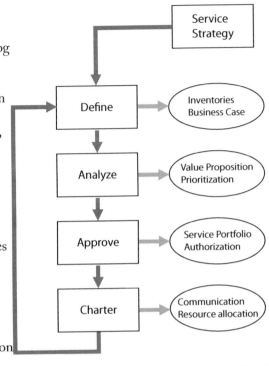

©Crown copyright 2007 - Reproduced under license from OGC

Figure 18 - Service Portfolio Management Activities

ACTIVITIES

When determining which services should be supported, Service Portfolio Management activities evaluate services to promote services to be designed based on the merits of the service. These activities include defining the service, analyzing the service, approving the service, and chartering the service.

This approach to what services should be considered for the Service Portfolio is to list all services with no constraints on resources, funding or time. In other words, list all services that could be provided if there were no limits to time, money, or resources. Constraints are then applied to these services and evaluated to determine which services should be provided and then prioritized. Once prioritized, the services that provide the most value and can be performed within our constraints are approved. These approved services are then assigned resources and chartered. Once chartered, the Service Level Package for this service is promoted to Service Design.

This process should occur regularly and include all services, not just those that are new. This regular review of services provides the opportunity for IT to determine where to apply resources and constraints. This regular review ensures that the right services are being offered that provide the right level of value to the business.

Define

The define method develops business cases for all of the services that would be offered if the organization had unlimited resources. This provides an overview of the needs of the business to achieve its business desired outcomes. This method is triggered by changes to the business that require defining new services or changes to existing services.

When defining a service, the definition of the service should be documented in terms of the value to the business. By focusing on business value, services are more likely to align to that value instead of "morphing" into some service that fails to align to the true customer needs.

Analyze

Since no organization has unlimited resources, the analyze method prioritizes the services into a set of services that can be offered through an acceptable use of resources. This maximizes the value of the Service Portfolio by offering high-value services to customers and either discontinuing or finding other ways to provide the lower value services. Over time, some services become commoditized so it is possible to find alternate sources for these services other than IT. These services are candidates for outsourcing.

Approve

When a service is approved, it is finalized in the Service Portfolio. This authorizes the service and authorizes the allocation of resources required for the service. When a service is not approved, it must be deliberately disapproved so there is no misconception regarding the service.

Charter

Chartering a service involves ensuring the decision for the service is clear and unambiguous. This communication triggers other activities such as inclusion of the service in the financial forecasts and triggering the processes in Service Design to design the service. Changes to services are also communicated through the charter method. Services identified for retirement triggers the service being discontinued through Service Transition.

Demand Management

Overview

Since services are perishable, delivery of services must match the demand for services or the services are wasted. Failure to anticipate increased demand can result in the inability to meet the demand and decrease the perception of value of customers. For example, with Geppetto Garcia's Inventory Control service, changes in product sales influence the demand for services. Therefore, if a change in sales is anticipated, a change in the service demand also can be anticipated.

Demand of the Gift Card Service

Mark Renner, CIO of Geppetto Garcia's, has been reading articles in the newspaper and industry magazines about the failures that have occurred in other businesses. One of the articles that he read involved an airline that left passengers stranded for several days due to the failure of one of their computer systems.[1]

Based on this information, Mark decides that he needs to determine when the demand of IT services fluctuate to ensure that the necessary resources are available to meet the demand. Mark uses concepts in the Demand Management process to determine that the year-end holiday season is when the gift card service will reach its highest demand. Mark has also identified other peaks in demand around Mother's Day and, for Geppetto's Sports Bar, there is another peak of gift card usage on Superbowl Sunday.

Based on these peak demand periods, Mark engages the Service Manager to determine if the gift card service will operate as expected during these high demand periods. The Service Manager will use this information to ensure that the design of the service takes into account these peak demand periods, and that the availability and capacity designs of

---

1   Comair computer crash could hurt the struggling airline. Charleston Gazette. December 29, 2004

the service are adequate. The Service Manager also ensures that these peak demand periods are documented in the Service Level Agreements by working closely with the Service Level Manager. These high priority periods are communicated throughout IT to ensure that the appropriate levels of support are anticipated.

KEY CONCEPTS

Demand Management is a collection of activities that strive to understand and influence customer demand for services and the provision of capacity to meet these demands. There are two aspects to Demand Management, strategic and tactical.

Tactical Demand Management involves influencing demand. One technique to influence demand is called differential charging. Differential charging is a technique that charges more or less for a service in an effort to balance demand or lessen peak demand. Cell phone companies, for example, provide reduced-cost calling in the evenings or on weekends. This technique is used to lower the demand during the daytime peak and transfer some of this demand, such as personal calls, to periods where there is excess capacity.

Strategic Demand Management involves analyzing Patterns of Business Activity (PBA's) to develop User Profiles (UP's) to anticipate demand for services. Both internal and external factors are reviewed to understand these patterns. To do this, the sources of demand are determined. Some of these sources include people, processes and applications. However, just about anything can be a source of demand. Inclement weather, for example, can be a source of demand for cell phone providers as the call volumes increase during periods of inclement weather.

These patterns then assist in determining cyclical changes in demand. Florists, for example, anticipate increased seasonal demand during Mother's Day and Valentine's Day, and prepare for increased manufacturing, sales and shipping during these times.

Once the sources of demand are determined, PBA's are developed that document patterns of demand. The PBA's consider the frequency, volume, location and duration of that demand. Once documented, these PBA's are under change control.

User Profiles (UP's) are then developed to document sources of demand and their individual patterns. These UP's combine one or more PBA's to determine overall patterns. For example, if we know that one user uses 5% of a server's CPU on Friday mornings between 8:00 AM and 10:00 AM, we can better determine how many servers are required for 100 users. This is very closely tied to the Capacity Management process described in the Service Design Processes chapter.

While it is documented in Service Strategy, Demand Management is prevalent in the other Service Lifecycle stages as well. In Service Strategy, Demand Management assists with the evaluation of the Service Portfolio to analyze service and forecast additional resources for services. Demand Management also works with Financial Management to influence demand through differential charging for services.

In Service Design, the design for services relies on the demand forecasts to optimize the design of the service. Proper design should anticipate the demand for the service to ensure that the service is "the right size" and not over or under-engineered.

In Service Design's Service Catalog Management process, the demand for the service is mapped in the Service Catalog. Lastly, Service Operation is affected by demand through resource scheduling and workload balancing of the service.

Financial Management

Overview

Financial Management is the process that provides financial input and output to other processes. The purpose of Financial Management is ensure proper funding of delivery of IT services, and to provide the business and IT with the quantification, in financial terms, of the value of the assets underlying the provisioning of services and the qualification of operational forecasting. This is done by identifying, documenting and agreeing on the value of services being received by the customer.

Financial Management at Geppetto Garcia's

Services are expensive to provide. In order to ensure that the right services are provided at the right cost, Mark Renner enlists the help of Susan Brockman, a financial analyst, to establish a Financial Management process within IT. Susan's new role comes with the responsibility to help IT and the business make better decisions with regard to the services that are provided by IT and how much money is spent on them.

In order to be effective, Susan must be able to account for all of the expenditures for each service and ensure that all expenditures are allocated appropriately to the correct service. This accounting provides the basis for further evaluation of the investments within a service. Using this information, Susan is better able to analyze the expenditures for a service and communicate these costs to the business.

Susan's desire, under Mark's direction, is to establish a charging system so that the business pays for the services that they utilize or ask for. Through a charging system, business becomes more responsible for their decisions, and the costs associated with those decisions. Value is also easier to communicate to the business because, once a charging system is in place, IT can communicate in the native language of the business - Finance. By communicating in this way, it is the desire of Mark Renner to be viewed in the eyes of the business as a Service Provider and increase the value that IT provides to the business.

BUSINESS VALUE

Financial Management communicates the value of services, usually by identifying costs. Without understanding the value of the service, it is difficult to make proper decisions regarding these services.

Other values to business include:

> Improved decision making
>
> Quicker and better evaluated change
>
> Improved Service Portfolio Management
>
> Improved financial compliance and control
>
> Improved operational control
>
> Communication of value capture and creation

KEY CONCEPTS

COST CLASSIFICATIONS

When accounting for services, the costs are categorized according to cost type. Cost types include labor costs, hardware costs, software costs, travel costs, etc. Costs are also classified by cost classification. These cost classifications include:

Direct versus Indirect

Direct costs are those that can be allocated entirely to a single customer or service. Direct costs support only that particular customer or service. Examples of direct costs are servers that only support one service, dedicated people to support a single service or other components that are dedicated to a single service.

Indirect costs, also known as "shared costs," support multiple services or customers. These shared costs should be allocated proportionally to the consumer of that service. For example, if a server is equally allocated to two services, the cost of the server should be allocated equally to each service. Other examples of indirect costs include the network infrastructure, utilities and the costs of the Service Desk.

Fixed versus Variable

Fixed costs are those costs which are paid regardless of use. These are costs that we must pay even if we do not use the product or service. Examples of fixed costs are servers, buildings, and salaries. These costs must be paid regardless of whether or not we use the server, occupy the building, or engage the people whose salaries we pay.

Variable costs are those costs that vary depending on the use of that service. Utilities are a common example of variable costs. Our utility costs vary depending on how much we use. Other examples include training costs, overtime costs and travel costs.

Capital versus Operational

Capital costs are those costs for an asset that is above some monetary value. Capital costs are often amortized from income taxes through the life of the cost. Examples of capital costs include buildings, vehicles and large servers.

Operational costs are those costs that are incurred for day-to-day operation of the service. These costs include salaries, printer consumable items, and utilities.

These cost classifications are not mutually exclusive in that a particular cost could be direct, variable, and operational. Using the above classifications, utilities, such as electricity, would be indirect, variable and operational costs. An expensive tape silo system to back up the entire infrastructure would be an indirect, fixed, and capital cost.

ACTIVITIES

The activities in Financial Management interact with processes in all other Service Lifecycle stages, even though they have been defined in Service Strategy. Briefly, the Financial Management activities include:

Service Valuation

Service Valuation strives to produce a value for services that is fair in order to obtain funding to support the service as an ongoing concern. This activity quantifies the funding of services expected from the business.

Demand Modeling

Demand Modeling quantifies the funding variations based on demand cycles and models demand behaviors. Demand Modeling works closely with Demand Management and Capacity Management to determine these demand cycles and costs associated with meeting demand.

Service Portfolio Management

Financial Management works closely with Service Portfolio Management to identify cost structures of services and to identify the costs of services.

Service Provisioning Optimization (SPO)

Service Provisioning Optimization (SPO) identifies costs and improves competitiveness of services through optimization of those costs.

Accounting

Accounting is the activity that records the consumption of service. Accounting also shows which consumer utilized the service and assigns those costs to the consumer.

Service Investment Analysis (SIA)

Service Investment Analysis improves investment decisions by analyzing the costs (investments) of a service. Service Investment Analysis also determines the standard expected return for a service using standard models.

Compliance

Compliance demonstrates that proper and consistent accounting methods are being deployed. With the recent legislation around Sarbanes-Oxley in the US, companies are required to conform to certain accounting practices or face penalties.

Variable Cost Dynamics (VCD)

Variable Cost Dynamics determines the variable sensitivity of services by analyzing the variables that impact the costs of services. The price of oil, for example, is a variable in many products and services that we buy in our everyday lives. Variable Cost Dynamics would be interested in determining the sensitivity of these products and services on the price of oil.

Planning Confidence

Planning Confidence is achieved by ensuring that the forecasts and other financial practices are correct within a significant margin of error. Through confidence in planning, assurances can be provided to ensure the proper funding is available for the delivery of services.

CHAPTER REVIEW

Service Strategy Processes

      Service Portfolio Management

      Demand Management

      Financial Management

Service Portfolio Management (SPM)

Responsible for maximizing the return on investment while managing risk

Service Portfolio

      Represents the complete set of services managed by the Service Provider.

      Includes three catalogs

            Service Pipeline

            Service Catalog

            Retired services

Activities

      Define

      Analyze

      Approve

      Charter

Demand Management

Collection of activities that strive to understand and influence customer demand for services and the provision of capacity to meet these demands

Tactical Demand Management

Uses differential charging to influence demand

Strategic Demand Management

Involves analyzing Patterns of Business Activity (PBA's) to develop User Profiles (UP's) to anticipate demand for services

Financial Management

Ensures proper funding of delivery of IT services and provides the business and IT with the quantification, in financial terms, of the value of the assets underlying the provisioning of services and the qualification of operational forecasting

Cost Classifications

Direct versus Indirect

Fixed versus Variable

Capital versus Operational

Activities

Service Valuation

Demand Modeling

Service Portfolio Management

Service Provisioning Optimization (SPO)

Accounting

Service Investment Analysis (SIA)

Compliance

Variable Cost Dynamics (VCD)

Planning Confidence

CHAPTER QUIZ

1.   What are the Service Strategy processes?

    a.   Service Portfolio Management
    b.   Service Catalog Management
    c.   Demand Management
    d.   Financial Management
    e.   Customer Management

2.   Match the process description with the correct process:

    a.   Financial Management
    b.   Demand Management
    c.   Service Portfolio Management

    i.   Ensure good stewardship of funds
    ii.   Makes decisions regarding services
    iii.   Ensure a steady demand exists for services

3.   What is the purpose of Service Portfolio Management (SPM)?

    a.   Manage the Service Portfolio
    b.   Maximize return at an acceptable risk
    c.   Ensure proper governance of IT resources
    d.   Match IT capabilities with demand for services

4.   What five questions should be answered by the Service Portfolio?

   a.   How should our resources and capabilities be allocated?
   b.   What are our strengths, weaknesses, priorities and risk?
   c.   How are the services provisioned?
   d.   How should they buy these services from us?
   e.   What is the availability of these services?
   f.   What are the pricing or chargeback models?
   g.   Why should a customer buy these services?

5.   The Service Pipeline is:

   a.   The list of services being considered as well as services in operation
   b.   The list of services being considered before they go into operation
   c.   The pipeline of requirements that should be considered for a new service
   d.   The demand for application development resources

6.   The Service Portfolio contains which three of the following?

   a.   Service Specifications
   b.   Service Pipeline
   c.   Service Catalog
   d.   Retired Services

7.   The methods for Service Portfolio Management (SPM) include:

   a.   Charter
   b.   Approve
   c.   Define
   d.   Analyze
   e.   Delegate

8. Arrange the methods for Service Portfolio Management in the proper order.

    a. Define
    b. Approve
    c. Charter
    d. Analyze

9. Which Demand Management focus involves the use of Patterns of Business Activity and User Profiles?

    a. Current
    b. Tactical
    c. Strategic
    d. Operational

10. Which Demand Management focus involves the use of differential charging to encourage customers to use IT services at less busy times?

    a. Tactical
    b. Strategic
    c. Current
    d. Operational

11. What are some possible sources of demand?

    a. People
    b. Processes
    c. Applications
    d. All of the above

12.   Purchasing a building typically has what cost classifications?

    a.   Direct, variable, and operational

    b.   Indirect, fixed, and capital

    c.   Direct, variable, and capital

    d.   Indirect, variable, and operational

13.   Service Desk staff salaries are usually considered to be variable, operational and _____ costs.

    a.   Tactical

    b.   Direct

    c.   Indirect

    d.   Overhead

Answers

1.	A, C, D
2.	A – i, B – iii, C – ii
3.	B
4.	A, B, D, F, G
5.	B
6.	B, C, D
7.	A, B, C, D
8.	A – D – B – C
9.	C
10.	A
11.	D
12.	B
13.	C

12

SERVICE DESIGN PROCESSES

OVERVIEW

The Service Design processes design services in a holistic manner based on the requirements, standards, and constraints in the Service Level Package (SLP) from Service Strategy.

The processes in Service Design are:

> Service Level Management
>
> Service Catalog Management
>
> Availability Management
>
> Capacity Management
>
> Information Security Management
>
> Supplier Management
>
> IT Service Continuity Management

Together, these processes consider all aspects of a service to ensure that the service is designed in a manner which can be transitioned to operation as effectively and efficiently as possible.

SERVICE LEVEL MANAGEMENT

GEPPETTO GARCIA'S

Mark Renner recognizes the importance of the IT services to meet the needs of the business. Without the business and its ability to operate effectively, IT would have no reason to exist. To ensure that the services are operating properly, Mark appoints a Service Level Manager, John Lawson.

It is John's job to ensure that the service requirements are well understood and document the levels of service required in Service Level Agreements (SLAs). John, as Service Level Manager, must negotiate the levels of service with the business. Once negotiated, the service is monitored in operation and the monitoring reports are reviewed periodically with the business.

When a service is not operating according to the needs of the business, the recognized improvements are made part of a Service Improvement Program (SIP). The Service Improvement Program is a formal program to improve a service. Any recognized improvement opportunities are recorded in the SIP for further action.

Overall, John Lawson is the central point of contact between the IT Service Provider and the business customer. John is the point of contact to communicate with the business through all stages of the Service Lifecycle. John also ensures the SLAs are properly documented and reviews occur with the business on a regular basis.

OVERVIEW

The Service Level Management (SLM) process is the conduit between IT and the business to represent the capabilities of IT to the business. SLM also strives to understand the needs of the business and communicate these needs so that services can be developed to meet these specific business needs.

PURPOSE

The purpose of Service Level Management is to negotiate, agree and document appropriate IT service targets with the representatives of the business, and then monitor and produce reports on the service provider's ability to deliver the agreed level of service in a consistent and professional manner. SLM is similar to an Account Management role with our service providers. For example, your organization's computer supplier has a designated Account Manager to ensure that your organization is satisfied with their computers. The Account Manager helps to resolve issues, as well as look for other areas where their products and services can add value to the organization.

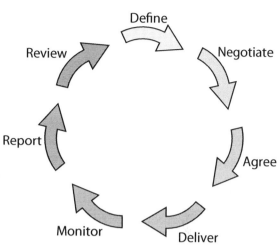

Figure 19 - Service Level Management Activities

When the requirements for new services, changes to service, or improvements to service are provided, SLM defines the new or changed service. Once defined, the service is negotiated with the business to obtain agreement to the level of service to be provided to meet the requirements.

The agreed service is then delivered. During delivery of the service, the service is monitored to identify gaps and deficiencies in the service. Periodically, this service is reviewed with the business and a new level of service is defined based on the findings in the review.

When a service first is introduced into the environment, the reviews of the service should be more frequent; perhaps quarterly. As the service matures, the review become less frequent but should be conducted at least annually.

GOALS AND OBJECTIVES

The goal of Service Level Management is to ensure than an agreed level of IT service is provided for all current IT services, and that future services are delivered to agreed achievable targets.

The objectives of Service Level Management include:

> Define, document, agree, monitor, measure, report and review the level of IT services provided

> Provide and improve the relationship and communication with the business and customers

> Ensure that specific and measurable targets are developed for all IT services

> Monitor and improve customer satisfaction with the quality of service delivered

> Ensure that IT and the customers have a clear and unambiguous expectation of the level of service to be delivered

> Ensure that proactive measures to improve the levels of service delivered are implemented wherever it is cost justifiable to do so

SLA's cannot be supported without the existence of Operational Level Agreements (OLA's). OLA's are agreements between internal organizations within an IT organization. The agreements define how internal IT organizations support each other in order to provide a specific level of service to the business.

Scope

Service Level Management provides a regular point of contact to the business by representing IT as a service provider. The business has a consistent point of contact to communicate their needs. SLM also manages the SLA's and provides reviews and negotiations for services to the business.

However, SLM also represents the needs of the business to IT. SLM produces Service Level Requirements (SLR's) that represent the business interests and requirements for IT to satisfy those interests or needs through services.

The scope of Service Level Management is to provide a service for the customer and improve that service based on customer needs. To do this, SLM must establish a relationship with the business and ensure that relationship is maintained. SLM is a document intensive process and ensures that Service Level Agreement, Service Level Requirements, Operational Level Agreements and Underpinning Contracts are established that support the service in accordance with business needs.

Working with the customer, Service Level Management strives to ensure that services meet the needs of the customer. It does this through providing high-quality services, preventing service failures proactively, reviewing SLAs and SLA breaches, investigating failures to services and coordinating a Service Improvement Program (SIP).

If SLM seems like it has a lot of responsibility, it does. However, SLM does not do all of these things alone. SLM works with other processes and works closely with other roles, such as the Service Owner, Service Level Manager and Continual Service Improvement Manager. SLM works with other processes within Service Design and through all stages of the Service Lifecycle to ensure quality services.

KEY CONCEPTS

Service Level Management is a document-intensive process. The documents produced and managed by SLM include those described below.

Service Level Agreements

A Service Level Agreement (SLA) is a written agreement between an IT service provider and the IT customer to define the key service targets and responsibilities of both parties. SLA's should be clear, concise, and emphasize the agreement between IT and the business. While SLA's must be adhered to, they should not be used as a way to hold either party ransom for failure to meet the agreement, but be focused on enhancing the performance of the business.

Service Level Agreements (SLA's) document the agreements for service between IT and the business. Many organizations approach these agreements generically as a "one-size-fits-all" agreement. By approaching SLA's in this manner, they fail to recognize the individual needs of the business unit, and are viewed as guidelines instead of agreements.

SLA's can be tailored to meet the specific needs of the business. They can be constructed by customer, by service, or as a combination of customer and service. IT Service Management strives to understand the needs of the business and meet those needs. SLA's document these needs and the provider's response to those needs.

Corporate Level SLA's

Corporate Level SLA's cover generic services common to all customers. These types of SLA's are constructed regardless of the business unit. Since almost all users use email, email could be covered under a Corporate Level SLA.

Customer Level SLA's

Customer Level SLA's address issues relevant for a particular customer. These SLAs are constructed with that specific customer in mind and addresses the requirements for that customer. An accounting organization, for example, may have a Customer Level SLA that addresses their needs for all services that they utilize from IT.

Service Specific SLA's

Service Specific SLA's cover the relevant issues of a specific service for a specific customer. For example, while all users use email, the Sales and Marketing organizations rely on email more than, say, manufacturing. A Service Specific SLA can be constructed for the email service that is different than the Corporate Level SLA to meet the specific needs of the Sales and Marketing organizations.

Multi-Level SLA's

SLA's can be multi-leveled. In our email example, the email service is covered for the entire organization through a Corporate Level SLA. Specific organizations with specific requirements may be covered by Customer Level or Service Specific SLA's constructed to meet their specific needs.

Service Level Requirement

A Service Level Requirement (SLR) is a Customer Requirement for an aspect of an IT service. SLR's are based on business objectives and are used to negotiate agreed Service Level targets. SLR's are provided to IT to communicate the requirements that must be met through services.

Operational Level Agreements

An Operational Level Agreement (OLA) is an agreement between internal parties to support services. OLA's document the responsibilities of the various groups in IT that are

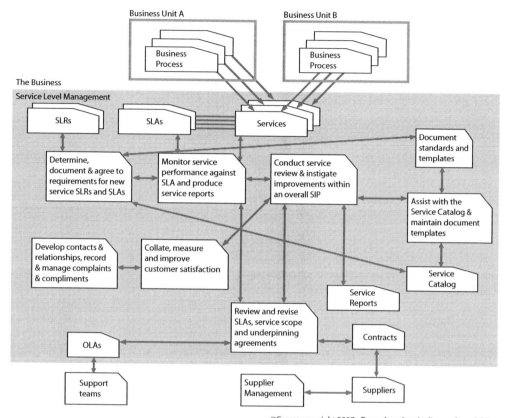

©Crown copyright 2007 - Reproduced under license from OGC

Figure 20 - Service Level Management Activities and Documents

responsible for support and maintenance of the services. Through OLA's, the organization understands their objectives and roles are more clearly defined.

Activities

SLM is responsible for representing the capabilities of IT to the business as well as representing the requirements of the business to IT. The activities involved include:

Determining, negotiating, documenting, and agreeing to requirements

Monitoring and measuring service performance

Improving customer satisfaction

Production of service reports

Conducting service reviews, and instigating improvements within an overall Service Improvement Plan (SIP)

Reviewing and revising SLA's, OLA's, contracts and other underpinning agreements

Developing, maintaining, and operating procedures for logging, auctioning, and resolving all complaints, and for logging and distributing compliments along with the Service Desk

Production of management information

Maintaining SLM templates and standards

SLM does not perform all these activities itself. SLM works closely with other processes to measure service performance. SLM specifically focuses on the communications with the customer and coordinates the activities of other processes to provide the customer reports and improvements to services.

Key Performance Indicators

Service Level Management metrics, or Key Performance Indicators (KPI's), can be objective or subjective. The subjective measurement is measured by improvements in customer satisfaction.

Objective measurements include:

Number or percentage of service targets being met

Number and severity of service breaches

Number of services with up-to-date SLA's

Number of services with timely reports and active reviews

Other metrics measure the quality of service and the business interface. These metrics include:

Quality of Service Metrics

Reduction in SLA targets missed

Because of OLA's

Because of external contracts

Reduction in SLA targets threatened

Reduction in costs of service provision

Reduction in costs of monitoring and reporting SLA's

Increase in speed of developing and agreeing to SLA's

Frequency of service reviews

Business Interface Metrics

Increased services covered by SLAs

Documented SLM procedures in place

Reduction in SLA's requiring corrections

Reduction in outstanding SLAs requiring annual renegotiation

Increase in OLA and external contract coverage

Evidence that issues with SLA's are followed up and addressed

Effective review of SLA, OLA and contract related breaches

Roles

The Service Level Manager is responsible for ensuring that the activities within Service Level Management are being performed. The Service Level Manager may be supported by Account Managers, Business Service Analysts or similar roles to ensure that services are being delivered to customers that are of high quality.

The specific Service Level Manager responsibilities include:

Ensuring that the current and future service requirements of customers are identified and understood

Ensuring that the current and future service requirements are documented in SLA and SLR documents

Negotiating and agreeing to levels of service

Negotiating and agreeing to OLA's

Assisting with the production of the Service Portfolio and the Service Catalog

Ensuring service reports are produced

Developing and maintaining relationships

Measuring, recording, analyzing and improving customer satisfaction

CHALLENGES

Service Level Management requires representing the abilities of IT to the business and representing the needs of the business to IT. To achieve this, SLM must straddle the line between IT and the business.

Other specific challenges to SLM include:

Identification of the service owner and customer can be difficult, which makes negotiation of the service difficult

SLA's are rushed to implementation without any prior experience

Differing levels and expectations between IT and the business

SLA targets are not realistic, achievable or cost effective

No way to monitor SLA's without proper monitoring

Lack of commitment to agreed SLA's

Lack of organizational understanding of the SLA process

Service Desk is not aware of existing SLA's

CRITICAL SUCCESS FACTORS

To be most efficient and effective, there are certain success factors that are critical within Service Level Management. These Critical Success Factors (CSF's) include:

The ability to manage the overall quality of IT services

The ability to deliver service at an affordable cost

The ability to manage the interface with business and users

Constant focus on the business

SERVICE CATALOG MANAGEMENT

OVERVIEW

Service Catalog Management is responsible for managing the Service Catalog. This is done by ensuring that: services within the Service Catalog are consistent with those in the Service Portfolio; the Service Catalog is accurate; and it is adequately protected and backed up.

The Service Catalog is one of the most important concepts in the effective and efficient operation of services. Just as no restaurant (or any other business for that matter) would be able to sell products and services without a menu of services, IT cannot either. One of the big issues with IT that the Service Catalog resolves is consistency. In most organizations, if the business requires something from IT, what they get is largely determined by who they ask and when they ask it. Without a consistent catalog of services, business and its users have no consistent view of what IT does. This dramatically lowers the perception of value of IT.

The Service Catalog provides a consistent communication of services that are available from IT. This consistency assists the business with understanding what services they can rely on in order to achieve their business desired outcomes. The other benefit of the Service Catalog is that it assists IT and IT staff to focus on the services they provide. It also tells IT why IT exists – to provide services and what those services are. Without a Service Catalog, the information regarding services is not reliable, consistent, or agreed upon.

PURPOSE

Service Catalog Management's purpose is to provide a single source of consistent information on all of the agreed upon services and ensure that it is widely available to those that are approved to access it. The way that Service Catalog Management provides this single source of consistent information is through the Service Catalog.

The goal of Service Catalog Management is to ensure that a Service Catalog is produced and maintained containing accurate information on all operational services and those being prepared to run operationally. The objective of Service Catalog Management is to manage the information contained within the Service Catalog and ensure that it is accurate and reflects the current details, status, interfaces and dependencies of all services that are being run or being prepared to run in the live environment.

Key Concepts

The Service Catalog contains the details of all operational services being provided or those being prepared for transition. The Service Catalog contains the Business Service Catalog and the Technical Service Catalog. The Business Service Catalog is the user view into the Service Catalog and provides information regarding the services that the user can request from IT. The Technical Service Catalog is the IT view of the services that are delivered to the customer, together with the supporting services and shared services. This is also referred to as the IT-to-IT Service Catalog.

Based upon information in the Business Service Catalog, when a user requests a service, or a change to a service, the request is fulfilled through the Request Fulfillment process in the Service Operations stage of the Service Lifecycle. The Business Service Catalog often is positioned along with the Service Desk to provide a greater level of service to the users.

Roles

The Service Catalog Manager is responsible for the production and maintenance of the Service Catalog. This includes ensuring that all operational services and transitioning services are recorded in the Service Catalog and the Service Catalog is consistent with the information in the Service Portfolio. The Service Catalog Manager reviews the Service Catalog periodically, particularly prior to release of a service into operation, to ensure that the Service Catalog is accurate. The Service Catalog Manager also ensures that the Service Catalog is adequately protected and backed up.

AVAILABILITY MANAGEMENT

OVERVIEW

Availability Management is the process that provides a point of focus and management for all availability related issues, relating to both services and resources, ensuring that availability targets in all areas are measured and achieved. Availability of services is extremely visible to customers and users. Therefore, Availability Management strives to understand the underlying aspects that contribute to availability of services, measure them, and find ways to improve availability.

The overriding principles that guide Availability Management include:

> Service availability is at the core of customer satisfaction and business success
>
> When services fail (not if), it is still possible to achieve business, customer and user satisfaction by responding to the failure in a way that influences perception of service
>
> Improvement can only begin after understanding how services support the business
>
> Service availability is only as good as the weakest link
>
> Availability is not just reactive, but proactive
>
> It is cheaper to design availability than to bolt it on later

PURPOSE

The purpose of Availability Management is to ensure that cost justifiable IT availability exists to match the current and future identified needs of the business.

Availability Management works closely with Service Level Management to understand these identified needs and also to support SLM reporting requirements.

KEY CONCEPTS

Availability

Availability is defined as *the ability of a service, component, or CI to perform its agreed function when required*. Also known as uptime, availability is calculated by dividing the total available time within a given time period by the agreed availability.

For example, suppose the server was down for 8 hours in a given work week. There are 168 hours in a work week. The server was available for 160 hours during the week (168 – 8). Dividing the 160 hours by the 168 total hours in the week results in .952. Multiplying this result by 100 results in calculating the percentage availability of 95.2%.

$$\text{Availability} = (168 - 8) / 168 * 100 = 95.2\%$$

Reliability

Reliability is defined as *a measure of how long a service, component, or CI can perform its agreed function without interruption*. Reliability is measured as Mean Time Between Service Interruptions (MTBSI) by dividing the time the service was available by the number of breaks. This shows the average time the service is running without failure.

Reliability is also measured by the Mean Time Between Failures (MTBF) by subtracting the total downtime from the available time and dividing by the number of breaks. This shows the average time between failures of the service.

Maintainability

Maintainability is defined as *a measure of how quickly and effectively a service, component, or CI can be restored to normal working after a failure*. Maintainability refers to how quickly a failure can be responded to. The speed in which a failure is responded depends on many things such as:

> Time to record the failure
>
> Time to respond

Time to resolve

Time to physically repair

Time to recover

Availability Management strives to understand and measure these contributory factors to downtime and find ways to reduce or eliminate these factors.

Maintainability is measured as Mean Time to Restore Service (MTRS) and is calculated by dividing the total downtime experienced by the number of outages. This reflects the average time to restore service following a failure.

Serviceability

Serviceability is defined as *the ability of a third-party supplier to meet the terms of their contract*. Serviceability plays a role in overall maintainability, and is also a key component of downtime to measure and control. This refers to the arrangements made with vendors to maintain and fix components that are part of a service.

VITAL BUSINESS FUNCTIONS

Every business organization has Vital Business Functions (VBF's). VBF's are the business critical elements of the business process that drive the business desired outcomes. VBF's are the elements of the business process that are more vital than other elements.

For example, the vital business function of an ATM machine is to dispense cash. A less vital function is the ability to produce a receipt. When you go to an ATM machine, your objective is to receive cash. The receipt is important, but not as important. If you can't get cash, the ATM machine shuts down. If you can't get a receipt, the ATM still functions, but in a limited capacity.

VBF's have different characteristics. These characteristics are:

High Availability

Characteristic of the IT service that minimizes or masks the effects of IT component failure

Fault Tolerance

Characteristic of an IT service to continue to operate after one of the components has failed

Continuous Operation

Characteristic of an IT service to eliminate planned downtime
Individual components may be down, but not affect the service

Continuous Availability

Characteristic of an IT service to achieve 100% availability masking planned and unplanned downtime

All IT organizations have limits on their resources, people, time, and money. Therefore, it is critical to work with business (through Service Level Management) to determine what the vital business functions are. Once the vital business functions are understood and documented, IT can prioritize where their limited resources are allocated to ensure that the maximum benefit is derived from these limited resources.

EXPANDED INCIDENT LIFECYCLE

Availability Management can be a tenacious process. Tenacity is needed in order to understand the contributing factors of downtime and reduce these factors.

The Expanded Incident Lifecycle (Figure 21) explores these contributing factors. When an incident occurs, it takes time to detect the incident. Some incidents are detected by monitoring tools, while others are reported by users. In a perfect world, no incidents would be reported by users, they would all be detected before the user was impacted and resolved with no impact. However, since we don't live in a perfect world and have limited resources, the focus should be on the highest priority services.

Detecting incidents is not the only contributing factor to downtime. It also takes time to diagnose incidents, repair incidents, recover incidents and restore services from an incidents.

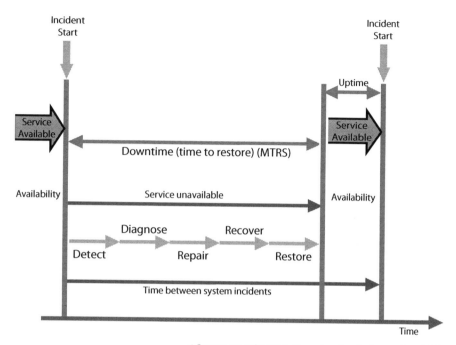

©Crown copyright 2007 - Reproduced under license from OGC

Figure 21 - The Expanded Incident Lifecycle

Detection

Detection of an incident occurs when the incident is reported to the Service Desk. This detection can be through monitoring tools (working with Event Management) or through a user call to the Service Desk. Ideally, every incident would be detected automatically. Detecting every single incident automatically would be very laborious and time consuming.

Diagnose

Determining the cause of an incident takes time, as well. Availability Management strives to reduce this time by working closely with other processes, such as Problem Management and Knowledge Management to ensure that scripts are developed to assist with the diagnostics, diagnostic tools are available, and the proper knowledge is contained within the Service Knowledge Management System to assist with this diagnostic. Incident handling staff also need to be trained to better understand how to diagnose an incident using these available tools and scripts.

Availability Management also strives to find other ways to minimize this contributing factor to downtime. While diagnostic activities may take a great deal of time, Availability Management may use resilience and redundancy techniques to ensure the service is still operational even though some part of it may have failed.

Repair

Repairing a service from an incidents involves many different activities that can only be partially defined prior to an incident occurring. Availability Management strives to ensure that the appropriate things are in place to ensure that repair to a service can be performed as quickly as possible. This includes designing response techniques into a service such as fail-over and fault tolerance to ensure that repair components are available and training or specialized personnel are available to repair the service.

Recover

Recovering the service involves bringing the service back to its operational state. This may involve ensuring that all components of the service are operating as expected and that the incident has been resolved.

Restore

Restoration of a service involves bringing a service back to its usable state. After recovery, there are times when data may need to be restored to ensure that users can continue to use the service as they did prior to the incident occurring.

ACTIVITIES

Availability Management is a process that has activities through many stages of the Service Lifecycle. These activities are both proactive and reactive. In the Service Design stage of the Service Lifecycle, the proactive activities include understanding the risk to the availability of a service, designing availability into a service, and improving availability through implementing cost-justifiable measures to counter the risk to availability.

In Service Transition, Availability Management is responsible for reviewing all new and changed services from an availability standpoint. Availability Management is also responsible for testing the availability mechanisms for services.

In Service Operation, the reactive activities of Availability Management include monitoring, measuring, analyzing, reporting, and reviewing service and component availability, as well as investigating all service and component unavailability and instigate remedial action.

Good Availability Management will be oblivious to which stage is currently being addressed, but will instead provide a holistic approach to the availability of services regardless of the Service Lifecycle.

Other key Availability Management activities include:

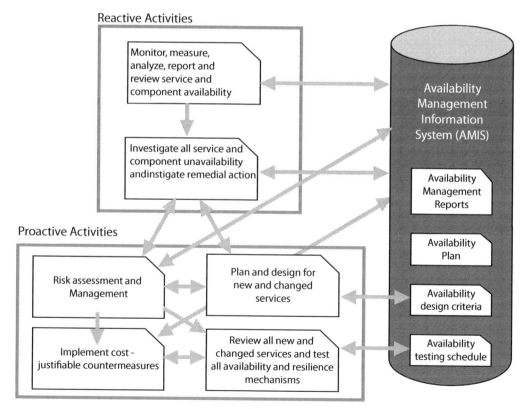

©Crown copyright 2007 - Reproduced under license from OGC

Figure 22 - Availability Management Activities

Determining the availability requirements from the business for a new or enhanced IT service and designing availability

Determining the VBF's in conjunction with the business and ITSCM

Determining the impact arising from component failure in conjunction with ITSCM

Providing additional resilience to prevent or minimize impact to the business

Defining targets for availability, reliability and maintainability

Establishing measures and reporting of availability, reliability and maintainability

Reviewing IT service and component availability and identifying unacceptable levels

Investigating the underlying reasons for unacceptable availability

Producing and maintaining an Availability Plan that prioritizes and plans IT availability improvements

AVAILABILITY MANAGEMENT INFORMATION SYSTEM

The Availability Management process is supported by the Availability Management Information System (AMIS). The AMIS is a system to store and maintain availability related information. The information contained and maintained in the AMIS includes Availability Management reports, availability plans, availability design criteria, and availability testing schedules.

ROLES

The Availability Manager is responsible for all of the activities in Availability Management and to provide a single focus on availability. The Availability Management process requires a disciplined and analytical approach to understand all of the contributing factors to availability and control them.

The Availability Manager works closely with the Service Level Manager to ensure that availability levels are being met according to the negotiated and agreed SLA's. The Availability Manager works closely with Technical Management, IT Operations Management and Applications Management teams to understand availability issues and design availability into services.

Capacity Management

Overview

Managing capacity requires balancing costs against resources to make efficient use of cost-justifiable resources. It also requires balancing supply with demand to ensure that the current and future demand can be met.

The Capacity Management process provides a single focus of management for all capacity and performance related issues, relating to both services and supply. Capacity Management works closely with Demand Management to understand and influence the demand against available resources.

Purpose

The purpose of Capacity Management is to ensure that cost-justifiable IT capacity for all areas of IT always exists and is matched to the current and future agreed needs of the business.

Key Concepts

Capacity Management involves more than just understanding the current capacity requirements, but understanding all aspects of demand for capacity. There are three sub-processes to Capacity Management that provide insight into these aspects.

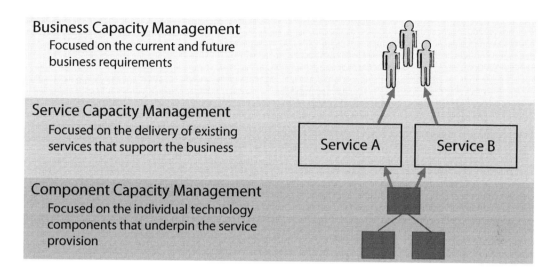

Business Capacity Management
Focused on the current and future
business requirements

Service Capacity Management
Focused on the delivery of existing
services that support the business

Service A   Service B

Component Capacity Management
Focused on the individual technology
components that underpin the service
provision

Figure 23 - Capacity Management Sub-Processes

BUSINESS CAPACITY MANAGEMENT

Business Capacity Management is focused on the current and future business requirements for capacity. For example, if the business were to state that they are going to
increase sales by 40% over the next year, Business Capacity Management must understand
how this change in business would influence capacity requirements for the service and the
underlying components.

SERVICE CAPACITY MANAGEMENT

Service Capacity Management is focused on ensuring that the current capacity can be
delivered by the service and that changes in demand can be delivered. There are many
examples in the news of companies that failed to anticipate demand for services and lost
business because of failures in delivering the required capacity. Well-established companies are not immune to this. A popular online auction site, online book retailer, and an
airline have made the news in the past because of interruptions in service due to lack of
capacity.

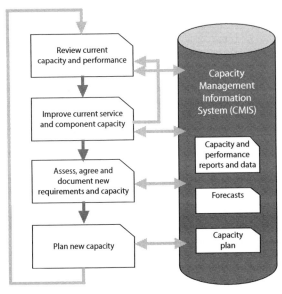

©Crown copyright 2007 - Reproduced under license from OGC

Figure 24 - Capacity Management Activities

COMPONENT CAPACITY MANAGEMENT

Component Capacity Management is familiar for most organizations because this sub-process monitors the individual component capacity. Typical monitoring includes monitoring disk space, CPU usage and memory usage. Component Capacity Management is also concerned with understanding the human resources required to meet demand for capacity.

Component Capacity Management metrics are often combined to reflect the service capacity.

ACTIVITIES

Capacity Management activities include reviewing current capacity and performance, improving current service and component capacity, assessing, agreeing and documenting new capacity requirements, and planning new capacity. Capacity Management is supported by the Capacity Management Information System (CMIS) that stores the forecasts, capacity plan, and capacity and performance reports and data.

ROLES

The Capacity Manager is responsible for all of the activities in Capacity Management, including understanding the requirements for capacity. The Capacity Manager's specific responsibilities include:

Ensuring there is adequate IT capacity

Identifying capacity requirements with the business along with Service Level Management

Understanding the current usage of the infrastructure

Performing sizing on new services

Forecasting future capacity requirements

Producing the Capacity Plan

Monitoring capacity

Analyzing capacity

Initiating any required tuning

Assessing new technology

Producing capacity reports

Being a focal point for all performance issues

Information Security Management

Overview

Organizations have become very security conscious. There have been various stories in the news lately about companies losing critical customer and employee data. This issue is becoming more exacerbated as we condense more and more information onto smaller devices. DVDs, thumb drives, and other media can store lots of information in a very small space. These devices are also very easy to lose if control measures are not in place.

Purpose

The purpose of the Information Security Management process is to align IT security with business security to ensure that information security is effectively managed. This security is achieved when:

Availability is met

The information is available and usable when required and systems can appropriately resist attacks, prevent and recover from failures

Confidentiality is met

The information is observed by or disclosed to only those who have a right to know

Integrity is met

Information is complete, accurate and protected against unauthorized modification

Authenticity is met

Business transactions, as well as information exchanges between enterprises, or with partners, can be trusted

KEY CONCEPTS

INFORMATION SECURITY FRAMEWORK

Information Security Management establishes a security framework to support the process and ensure that security encompasses the entire lifecycle of the service.

At the core, the Information Security Management framework consists of:

> Establishing specific security policies that address the strategy, control and regulation of security
>
> Establishing a set of controls to support the policies
>
> Developing a comprehensive security strategy that is closely linked to business objectives, strategies and plans
>
> Establishing an effective security organizational structure

This core supports the following components of the framework:

> Managing security risks
>
> Monitoring processes to ensure compliance
>
> All IT Service Management processes must be monitored to ensure compliance with security requirements
>
> Training and awareness of strategy and plans
>
> Establishing a communications strategy to ensure that security requirements and policies are known and understood
>
> Information Security Management System

Information Security Management is supported by the Information Security Management System (ISMS). The ISMS records all security related information, including standards, management information, procedures and guidelines.

POLICIES

Information Security Management develops an overall Information Security Policy. This policy drives all activities and refers to specific underpinning security policies. The Information Security Policy must have the support of top management to ensure that it can be enforced and promote adherence to the policies.

Specific underlying policies depend on the unique organization, but some of the policies to consider include:

>Use and misuse of IT assets
>
>Access control policy
>
>Password control policy
>
>Email policy
>
>Internet policy
>
>Anti-virus policy
>
>Information classification policy
>
>Document classification policy
>
>Remote access policy
>
>Supplier access policy
>
>Asset disposal policy

ACTIVITIES

As show in Figure 25, the security framework involves five key activity groups. These activity groups are Control, Planning, Implement, Evaluate and Maintain.

Control

Security control is provided though the development and communication of policies and procedures, understanding security requirements, and imple-

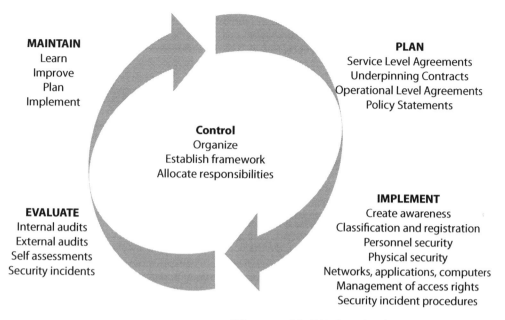

Figure 25 - Security Management Framework

menting an organization that can manage security effectively and allocating responsibilities for security.

Planning

Planning for security is driven by the requirements contained in the security chapter of the Service Level Agreements (SLA's). The SLA contains any security requirements from the business that are above and beyond the standard organizational security.

Planning for security also includes planning and reviewing the underpinning contracts, Operational Level Agreements (OLA's) and policy statements to determine if modifications are necessary to accommodate the security requirements.

Implement

The implementation activities involve creating awareness about security, developing a classification and registration system for security and data, and securing the networks, applications, computer and other components for a service. Implementation also involves establishing security for personnel and physical security, as well as managing access rights.

Security Management also reviews incidents from Incident Management to resolve security related incidents.

Evaluate

The evaluation activities for Information Security Management include internal and external audits and self assessments. Internal audits involve an IT security specialist group to audit the security of the organization. External audits involve hiring an external group to audit the security of the organization. Self assessments involve the organization assessing its own security usually using checklists provided by Information Security Management.

Security incidents are also evaluated in this activity group to evaluate the actions to take regarding security related incidents.

Maintain

The maintenance activities involve understanding what was found in the evaluation activities, learning from those findings to improve security, and implementing improvements to the organization.

ROLES

The Security Manager is responsible for ensuring that all activities in the Information Security Management process are performed, for maintaining the Information Security Policy and supporting policies and making sure that these policies are adhered to. The Security Manager may have security teams with specific responsibilities for security activities. These security team structures are dependent on the overall organization.

The specific Security Manager responsibilities include:

> Establishing and maintaining the Information security policy and supporting policies
>
> Communicating the information security policy
>
> Enforcing the information security policy
>
> Identifying and classifying IT and information assets by determining the level of control and security required

Performing a security risk analysis with Availability Management and IT Service Continuity Management

Responding to security breaches

Reducing security-related incident volumes

Assessing impact of changes on security

Testing security

Security reviews

Ensuring confidentiality, integrity and availability of services including external vendors and suppliers

Being a focal point for all security issues

SUPPLIER MANAGEMENT

PURPOSE

Supplier Management, commonly referred to as Vendor Management, is responsible for obtaining value for money from suppliers and to ensure that suppliers perform to the targets contained within their contracts and agreements while conforming to all the terms and conditions. Supplier Management formally manages the suppliers in a way that provides value to the organization based on the commitments and contracts with the suppliers.

GOAL AND OBJECTIVES

The goal of Supplier Management is to manage suppliers and the services they supply to provide seamless quality of IT service to the business, ensuring value for money is obtained.

The objectives of Supplier management are to:

> Obtain value for money from suppliers and contracts
>
> Align underpinning contracts and agreements with suppliers to business needs
>
> Aligns to SLA's and SLR's
>
> Manage relationship with suppliers
>
> Manage supplier performance
>
> Negotiate and agree to contracts with suppliers through the entire life-cycle
>
> Maintain a supplier policy and supporting Supplier and Contract Database (SCD)

KEY CONCEPTS

UNDERPINNING CONTRACTS

Underpinning Contracts, or contracts, are the agreements between IT and IT's vendors. The underpinning contracts are maintained by Supplier Management to ensure that the contracts are providing the right level of support for services.

While contracts are agreed to by the Supplier Management process, Service Level Management will be involved in reviewing the contracts to ensure that the contracts provide the appropriate support for the SLA's. Service Level Management works with the Supplier Management process, but leaves the actual negotiation of the contract to the Supplier Management process.

SUPPLIER AND CONTRACTS DATABASE (SCD)

The Supplier and Contracts Database (SCD) contain all the records for suppliers and their associated contracts. The SCD also contains the list of all services and/or products supplied by the supplier.

All activities in Supplier Management reference this database and ensures that the database is accurate and timely. With an accurate Supplier and Contracts Database, important dates are not missed and suppliers are well managed. If contract deadlines are missed or delayed, it could result in added expense and penalties.

ACTIVITIES

Supplier Management involves a set of integrated activities to develop strategies and evaluate and manage suppliers.

Supplier Strategy and Policy

Supplier Management develops strategies and policies with regard to the suppliers. This strategy and policy provides overriding guidelines for the remaining activities.

Evaluation of New Suppliers and Contracts

When new suppliers are considered, Supplier Management evaluates the new suppliers and the proposed contracts to ensure that they conform to the strategy and policy set forth.

Establish New Suppliers and Contracts

Upon acceptance of new suppliers and contracts, these suppliers and contracts are established in the Supplier and Contracts Database (SCD) to ensure that they can be properly managed.

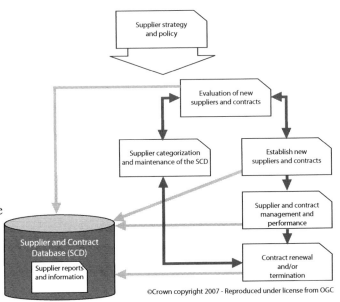

©Crown copyright 2007 - Reproduced under license from OGC

Figure 26 - Supplier Management Activities

Supplier and Contract Management and Performance

Periodically, the suppliers and contracts are evaluated to ensure that they are in compliance with the obligations agreed to in the contract. This evaluation also ensures that the organization is conforming with its obligations to the suppliers and contracts as well.

Contract Renewal and/or Termination

When contracts are scheduled to terminate, the contract is reviewed to determine if it should be renewed or terminated. Termination of a contract involves formal procedures to ensure that all terms and obligations of the contract have been satisfied by both the supplier and the organization.

Supplier Categorization and Maintenance of the SCD

The Supplier and Contracts Database (SCD) is a location to store all of the records regarding the suppliers and the contracts for the suppliers. When a new supplier and contract have been established, the supplier and/or contract should be categorized in the SCD. The SCD also requires periodic maintenance to prune or archive old records and ensure that the SCD is performing its objectives.

Categorization of the supplier and the contract reflects the relative importance of the supplier or contract to the organization. This categorization is determined by the risk and impact of the supplier for non-performance, and the value and importance of the supplier or contract. Some suppliers are commodity suppliers. Commodity suppliers are those that provide low-value and low-risk services, such as providing paper and toner for printers. Paper and toner can easily be obtained through other suppliers.

Operational suppliers are those suppliers who have a low impact, but medium or high risk to the organization or those that provide medium or high value services, but are low risk. Examples of operational suppliers include the utility providers such as electricity, gas and water. Tactical suppliers are those suppliers that have higher risk and value to the organization. These suppliers may be contracted to provide short to medium term solutions such as contract project work.

The strategic suppliers are those suppliers that provide high value and are high risk if they cannot perform. These suppliers are contracted to provide services that are core to the organization. These strategic suppliers usually have relationships with the higher levels of the organization's executive staff.

The purpose of categorizing suppliers is to ensure that the most important suppliers are provided with the support and attention that they require to be successful. This isn't to say that commodity suppliers should be ignored, but that the most attention should be given to where it is most needed.

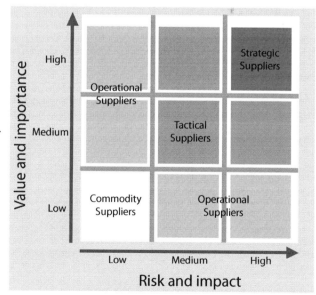

©Crown copyright 2007 - Reproduced under license from OGC

Figure 27 - Supplier Categorization

ROLES

The Supplier Manager, often someone from the Procurement group, ensures that vendors are appropriately reviewed and selected, and maintains all the documentation, including proposals and contracts, pertaining to the vendor. The Supplier Manager also has the responsibility of working closely with Service Level Management to ensure that SLM processes and documentation are updated accordingly, as well as report supplier performance against the SLA's.

IT Service Continuity Management

Overview

IT Service Continuity Management (ITSCM) is responsible for maintaining the necessary ongoing recovery capability within the IT services and their supporting components in the event of a disaster. While most organizations have disaster recovery processes in place, the differentiator between disaster recovery and IT Service Continuity Management is that ITSCM is tightly integrated with the Business Continuity Plan (BCP).

IT Service Continuity Management achieves the recovery capability by introducing risk reduction measures and introducing recovery options. ITSCM requires all members of the organization to support it effectively. ITSCM also must have support from senior management to ensure that plans are in place, resources are allocated, and funds are available to provide the recovery capability.

ITSCM strives to align recovery of the IT technical and services infrastructure based on the priority of business processes. In Availability Management, the concept of Vital Business Function (VBF's) was explored. These VBF's play a major part of ITSCM as well. ITSCM strives to understand these VBF's to ensure that services are recovered according to business priority.

Purpose

IT Service Continuity Management supports the overall Business Continuity Management process by ensuring that the required IT technical and service facilities can be resumed within required and agreed business time scales.

Other objectives of ITSCM include:

>Maintain a set of IT Service Continuity Plans and IT recovery plans that support the overall Business Continuity Plans (BCP's)
>
>Complete regular Business Impact Analysis (BIA) activities
>
>Conduct regular Risk Analysis and Management activities in conjunction with Availability Management
>
>Provide advice and guidance to other areas of the business
>
>Ensure that continuity and recovery mechanisms are in place
>
>Assess the impact of all changes
>
>Improve availability of services through proactive measures
>
>Negotiate and agree to required contracts with suppliers in conjunction with Supplier Management

ACTIVITIES

ITSCM begins with input from Business Continuity Management (BCM). Business Continuity Management develops a business continuity strategy and resultant business continuity plans. ITSCM develops its requirements and strategy, and implements ITSCM with respect to this business strategy and plans.

As shown in Figure 28, the ITSCM activities are organized around a series of stages. These stages are:

Initiation

The Initiation stage recognizes the need to establish a project to develop an ITSCM plan. This stage allocates resources to begin development of the Requirements and Strategy.

Requirements and Strategy

The Requirements and Strategy stage works closely with the Business Continuity Management (BCM) process to perform a Business Impact Analysis (BIA). The BIA considers the business processes and prioritizes these processes by the impact of these processes being interrupted.

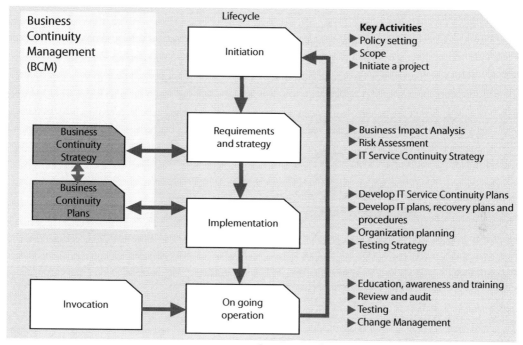

©Crown copyright 2007 - Reproduced under license from OGC

Figure 28 - IT Service Continuity Management Activities

From this BIA, a risk assessment is conducted to determine the risks to the business. The ITSCM strategy is developed to provide guidance for the remaining stages.

Implementation

The Implementation stage is where the work is performed to create an ITSCM plan and put it into operation. This stage involves developing the ITSCM plans, and the IT plans, recovery plans and procedures to support the ITSCM plan. Organizational planning considers the support requirements from the organization to implement and provide ongoing support of the ITSCM plan. Testing strategy is also developed that involves testing the plan upon initial implementation and then providing ongoing testing of the plan at least annually.

Ongoing Operation

Once the plan has been implemented, it requires ongoing operation for the activities to remain aligned with the needs of the business. Because the ITSCM plan is one that we hope is not ever invoked, it runs the risk of becoming stale and out of date. Ongoing education, awareness and training are provided to ensure that the plan is current and has organizational awareness.

Through Operation, the plan is periodically reviewed and audited for any changes in business requirements for consideration and updates to the plan. At least annually, the plan is tested to identify any gaps and opportunities for improvement.

Change Management has special considerations with ITSCM. Changes have the potential to impact the ITSCM plan. When a change is introduced into the live environment, the change is also duplicated in the recovery or failover environment to ensure that the environments remain consistent.

Invocation

The Invocation stage is triggered when a major failure or disaster has occurred that warrants invoking the IT Service Continuity plan. When the plan is invoked, the plan is carried out as practiced and tested. During invocation, there should be no major decisions to make, as these decisions have been pre-determined and tested.

ROLES

The ITSCM Manager is responsible for all activities and ensuring that ITSCM plans, procedures and the process aligns with the business requirements. The ITSCM Manager works closely with the Service Level Manager to understand the business requirements and ensure these requirements are documented in the Service Level Agreement's Continuity Chapter.

The specific responsibilities of the IT Service Continuity Manager are:

> Performing the Business Impact Analysis (BIA)
> Implementing and maintaining the ITSCM process
> Ensuring that ITSCM activities are aligned with business processes
> Performing risk assessment and management
> Testing ITSCM with post-mortem reviews

Ensuring organizational preparedness

Reviewing ITSCM plans at least annually

Negotiating and managing contacts with 3rd party vendors

Assessing changes for their impact on ITSCM

CHAPTER REVIEW

Service Design Processes

> Service Level Management
>
> Service Catalog Management
>
> Availability Management
>
> Capacity Management
>
> Information Security Management
>
> Supplier Management
>
> IT Service Continuity Management

Service Level Management

Purpose

> Negotiate, agree and document appropriate IT service targets with the representatives of the business, and then monitor and produce reports on the service provider's ability to deliver the agreed level of service in a consistent and professional manner.

Service Level Agreement (SLA)

> Written agreement between an IT service provider and the IT customer to define the key service targets and responsibilities of both parties.

Corporate Level SLA's

> Cover generic services common to all customers.

Customer Level SLA's

> Addresses issues relevant for a particular customer.

Service Specific SLA's

> Cover the relevant issues for a specific service for a specific customer.

Service Level Requirement (SLR)

Customer requirement for an aspect of an IT service.

Operational Level Agreement (OLA)

Agreement between internal parties to support services.

Activities

Determining, negotiating, documenting and agreeing to requirements

Monitoring and measuring service performance

Improving customer satisfaction

Production of service reports

Conducting service review and instigating improvements within an overall Service Improvement Plan (SIP)

Reviewing and revising SLA's, OLA's, contracts and other underpinning agreements

Developing, maintaining, and operating procedures for logging, auctioning, and resolving all complaints, and for logging and distributing compliments along with the Service Desk

Production of management information

Maintaining SLM templates and standards

Roles

Service Level Manager

Responsible for ensuring that the activities within Service Level Management are being performed.

Service Catalog Management

Purpose

To provide a single source of consistent information on all of the agreed upon services and ensure that it is widely available to those that are approved to access it.

Availability Management

Purpose

To ensure that cost justifiable IT availability exists to match the current and future identified needs of the business.

Definitions

Availability	The ability of a service, component, or CI to perform its agreed function when required
Reliability	A measure of how long a service, component, or CI can perform its agreed function without interruption
Maintainability	A measure of how quickly and effectively a service, component, or CI can be restored to normal working after a failures
Serviceability	The ability of a third-party supplier to meet the terms of their contract
Vital Business Functions (VBFs)	The business critical elements of the business process that drive the business desired outcomes

VBF's Characteristics

High Availability

Fault Tolerance

Continuous Operation

Continuous Availability

Availability Management Information System (AMIS)

A system to store and maintain availability related information.

Roles

Availability Manager

Responsible for all of the activities in Availability Management and to provide a single focus on availability.

Capacity Management

Purpose

To ensure that cost-justifiable IT capacity for all areas of IT always exists and is matched to the current and future agreed needs of the business.

Business Capacity Management

Focused on the current and future business requirements for capacity.

Service Capacity Management

Focused on ensuring that the current capacity can be delivered by the service and that changes in demand can be delivered.

Component Capacity Management

Focused on ensuring that the component capacity is sufficient to deliver the service.

Roles

Capacity Manager

Responsible for all of the activities in Capacity Management, including understanding the requirements for capacity.

Information Security Management

Purpose

To align IT security with business security to ensure that information security is effectively managed.

Activities

Control

Planning

Implement

Evaluate

Maintain

Roles

Security Manager

Responsible for ensuring that all the activities in the Information Security Management process are performed, for maintaining the Information Security Policy and supporting policies, and making sure that these policies are adhered to.

Supplier Management

Purpose

To obtain value for money from suppliers and to ensure that suppliers perform to the targets contained within their contracts and agreements while conforming to all the terms and conditions.

Underpinning Contracts

Agreements between IT and IT's vendors.

Supplier and Contracts Database (SCD)

Contains all the records for suppliers and their associated contracts.

Activities

Supplier Strategy and Policy

Evaluation of New Suppliers and Contracts

Establish New Suppliers and Contracts

Supplier and Contract Management and Performance

Contract Renewal and/or Termination

Supplier Categorization and Maintenance of the SCD

Roles

Supplier Manager

Ensures that vendors are appropriately reviewed and selected, as well as maintains all the documentation, including proposals and contracts, pertaining to the vendor.

IT Service Continuity Management

Purpose

Supports the overall Business Continuity Management process by ensuring that the required IT technical and service facilities can be resumed within required and agreed business time scales.

Activities

Initiation

Requirements and Strategy

Implementation

Ongoing Operation

Invocation

Roles

IT Service Continuity Manager

Responsible for all activities and ensuring that ITSCM plans, procedures and the process aligns with the business requirements.

CHAPTER QUIZ

1. List the activities of Service Level Management (SLM) in the correct order.

    a. Negotiate
    b. Define
    c. Agree
    d. Review
    e. Monitor
    f. Deliver

2. Service Level Management is a cyclical process.

    a. True
    b. False

3. Service Level Management (SLM) represents IT as a service provider and:

    a. represents business interests to IT
    b. manages the Service Desk
    c. guarantees delivery of services to the customer
    d. improves services based on a continual improvement focus

4. Match the following documents with their definitions.

    a. Service Level Agreement
    b. Service Level Requirement
    c. Operational Level Agreement

    i.   Written agreement between IT and the customer
    ii. Agreement between internal parties to support services
    iii. Customer requirements

5. Service Level Agreements should be consistent throughout the organization for all customers for all services.

    a. True

    b. False

6. What are the three structures of Service Level Agreements?

    a. Corporate Level SLA's

    b. User Level SLA's

    c. Customer Level SLA's

    d. Service Specific SLA's

7. The two views into the Service Catalog include:

    a. Vendor Catalog

    b. Business Service Catalog

    c. User Service Catalog

    d. Technical Service Catalog

8. Availability Management provides a point of focus and management for all availability related issues.

    a. True

    b. False

9. Availability efforts are always reactive.

    a. True

    b. False

10. The term given for the business critical elements of a business process is called what?

    a.   Business Priority

    b.   Critical Business Activity

    c.   Critical Business Function

    d.   Vital Business Function

    e.   Core Service

11. What is the characteristic of the IT service that minimizes or masks the effects of IT component failure?

    a.   Continuous Availability

    b.   Continuous Operation

    c.   High Availability

    d.   Fault Tolerance

12. What is the characteristic of the IT service to continue to operate after one of the components has failed?

    a.   Continuous Availability

    b.   Fault Tolerance

    c.   Continuous Operation

    d.   High Availability

13. What is the characteristic of an IT service to eliminate planned downtime?

    a.   Continuous Operation

    b.   High Availability

    c.   Fault Tolerance

    d.   Continuous Availability

14. What is the characteristic of an IT service to achieve 100% availability masking planned and unplanned downtime?

   a.   Continuous Availability

   b.   High Availability

   c.   Fault Tolerance

   d.   Continuous Operation

15. What is the name given for the system that holds Availability Management reports, the Availability Plan, Availability Design Criteria and the Availability Testing Schedule?

   a.   Configuration management System (CMS)

   b.   Availability Management Information System (AMIS)

   c.   Capacity Management Information System (CMIS)

   d.   Availability Support System

16. What is the term used for the ability of a service, component or CI to perform its agreed function when required?

   a.   Availability

   b.   Reliability

   c.   Maintainability

   d.   Serviceability

17. What is the term used for the measure of how long a service, component, or CI can perform its agreed function without interruption?

   a.   Serviceability

   b.   Maintainability

   c.   Availability

   d.   Reliability

18. What is the term used for the measure of how quickly and effectively a service, component or CI can be restored to normal working after a failure?

    a.   Maintainability

    b.   Availability

    c.   Reliability

    d.   Serviceability

19. What is the term used for the ability of a third-party supplier to meet the terms of their contract?

    a.   Availability

    b.   Serviceability

    c.   Reliability

    d.   Maintainability

20. What process provides a point of focus and management for all capacity and performance related issues, relating to both services and resources?

    a.   Demand Management

    b.   Capacity Management

    c.   Availability Management

    d.   Service Level Management

21. Match the sub processes of Capacity Management with their descriptions.

    a.   Focus on current and future identified needs of the business

    b.   Focus on the delivery of existing services

    c.   Focus on the individual technology components

    i.   Component Capacity Management

    ii.   Service Capacity Management

    iii.   Business Capacity Management

22. What is the name given for the system that holds forecasts, the Capacity Plan and capacity and performance reports and data?

 a. Capacity Management Information System (CMIS)

 b. Configuration Management System (CMS)

 c. Availability Support System

 d. Availability Management Information System (AMIS)

23. What is the name of the process that aligns IT security with business security to ensure information security is effectively managed?

 a. Access Management

 b. Information Security Management

 c. Availability Management

 d. Network Security Management

24. Match the term with its description.

 a. Information is available and usable when required

 b. Information is available to only those who have a right to know

 c. Information is complete, accurate and protected

 d. Transactions can be trusted

 i. Integrity

 ii. Authenticity

 iii. Confidentiality

 iv. Availability

25. What is the name given for the system that holds security related standards, management, procedures and guidelines?

   a.   Configuration Management System (CMS)
   b.   Availability Support System
   c.   Information Security Management System (ISMS)
   d.   Availability Management Information System (AMIS)

26. What are the three main characteristics of the Information Security Policy?

   a.   It refers to specific underpinning security policies
   b.   It drives all security activities
   c.   It is managed directly by the CIO
   d.   It has the top support of management

27. What is the name of the database that supports all activities in Supplier Management?

   a.   Supplier Management Information System (SMIS)
   b.   Vendor Management Database (VMD)
   c.   Configuration Management Database (CMDB)
   d.   Supplier and Contracts Database (SCD)

28. What is the name of the process that is responsible for maintaining the ongoing recovery capability within the IT services and their supporting components?

   a.   IT Service Continuity Management
   b.   IT Service Risk Management
   c.   Disaster Management
   d.   Risk Management

29. IT Service Continuity management activities cannot be effective unless they are linked to what business process?

   a. Business Continuity Management

   b. Business Disaster Management

   c. Business Risk Management

   d. Business Strategy

Answers

1. B, A, C, F, E, D
2. A
3. A
4. A – i, B – iii, C – ii
5. B
6. A, C, D
7. B, D
8. A
9. B
10. D
11. C
12. B
13. A
14. A
15. B
16. A
17. D
18. A
19. B
20. B
21. A – iii, B – ii, C – i
22. A
23. B
24. A – iv, B – iii, C – i, D – ii
25. C
26. A, B, D
27. D
28. A
29. A

13

SERVICE TRANSITION PROCESSES

OVERVIEW

The Service Transition stage of the Service Lifecycle involves transitioning the design of a service to an operational service. The processes involved in this stage are focused on reducing risk during transition, as well as improving ongoing control of the service.

The Service Transition processes include:

> Change Management
>
> Service Asset and Configuration Management
>
> Release and Deployment Management
>
> Knowledge Management

Change Management

Overview

Change Requests can be generated from any place in the organization for a number of reasons. Some proactive reasons for a Change Request can be reduction of costs, productivity improvements, quality improvements, service improvements and functionality improvements. Reactive reasons for Change Requests can be to resolve errors or to adapt to a changing environment.

The Change Management process activities are triggered by Requests for Change (RFC's). RFC's are a mechanism to request a change to be made to a service.

Purpose

The purpose of Change Management is to ensure that standardized methods and procedures are used for efficient and prompt handling of all changes. Change Management also ensures that all changes to service assets and configuration items are recorded in the Configuration Management System (CMS). All of these activities ensure that Change Management optimizes overall business risk.

Without an effective Change Management process in place, an organization cannot effectively control changes. This results in a low change success rate and unplanned outages. Without the ability to plan for changes, an organization will experience a high number of emergency changes. In effect, unauthorized changes become the norm. An effective Change Management process strives for no unauthorized changes in the environment but an environment where all changes are managed.

Change Management ensures that any change to a service follows a well-defined, documented, measurable, and consistent process. This doesn't mean that all changes must follow the same path through the process, but that the types of changes are understood and have paths through the process.

The most difficult part of Change Management is to understand the types (or classes) of change that an organization implements on a regular basis. By classifying the types of change that an organization encounters, these changes can be modeled in a Change Management process in a way that all changes can be anticipated and supported with this process.

VALUE TO BUSINESS

Changes are inherently risky. Proper Change Management balances the risk with the expected return of the change to ensure that the risk is worth the value associated with the change.

Specific values to business include:

> Improved prioritization and response to change proposals
>
> Improved implementation of changes that meet service requirements
>
> Improved contribution to governance, legal, contractual and regulatory requirements
>
> Reduction in failed changes, service disruption, defects and re-work
>
> More prompt delivery of changes
>
> Changes are tracked through the service lifecycle and to the assets of the customers
>
> Better estimations of quality, time and cost of change
>
> Improved risk management
>
> Improved productivity
>
> Reduction in the Mean Time to Restore Service (MTRS) through quicker corrective actions

KEY CONCEPTS

Regardless of the type or source of change, all changes must follow a process with specific procedures to ensure that all changes are recorded, evaluated, authorized, prioritized, planned, tested, implemented and documented. A proper Change Management process ensures that these overriding objectives are met for every change.

7 R's OF CHANGE MANAGEMENT

Every change must be evaluated to answer the following seven questions. The following seven questions reflect the 7 R's of Change Management.

Who RAISED the change?

This identifies the person that requested the change. This person is often also a stakeholder for the change.

What is the REASON for the change?

A business case should accompany the change to ensure that there is a valid business reason for performing this change.

What is the RETURN required from the change?

This identifies what is expected from the change.

What are the RISKS involved in the change?

Every change should involve a risk assessment to ensure that as many risks as possible are identified and managed to either reduce the likelihood of that risk occurring or mitigating the impact should the risk occur.

What RESOURCES are required to deliver the change?

This identifies the resources required, such as funding, people and technology.

Who is RESPONSIBLE for the build, test, and implementation of the change?

This identifies the individuals who are expected to perform the activities involved in the change.

What is the RELATIONSHIP between this change and other changes?

Changes often impact one another, particularly when implemented at the same time. This identifies these interrelationships to reduce the risk associate with the change.

CHANGE PRIORITY

When changes are classified, they are assigned a priority. The priority is based on the urgency and impact. The urgency refers to how long the implementation can afford to be delayed and is often a subjective measure based on the requestor's needs and/or wants.

The impact is the beneficial change to the business that will follow from a successful implementation, or the degree of damage and cost to the business due to the error that the change will correct. Impact should be measured by disruption to the business defined outcomes, such as revenue.

Some organizations measure their impact by business desired outcomes other than revenue. For large city police departments, for example, communications failures are high impact. Other organizations may measure impact by loss of life or limb, or threat to the populace.

These two things, urgency and impact, are evaluated to determine the priority of a Change, Incident, or Problem.

Change Advisory Board

The Change Advisory Board (CAB) is the name provided for the group of stakeholders that meet to evaluate high impact requests for change. The CAB consists of representatives from IT and the business, and includes customers, users, IT Management, IT staff, consultants and vendors, if necessary. The attendees of a CAB meeting depend on the specific change being considered.

Potential CAB members

> Change Manager (chairs the CAB)
>
> Customers
>
> User managers
>
> User group representatives
>
> Applications developers/maintainers
>
> Specialists/technical consultants
>
> Services and operations staff
>
> Service Desk
>
> Test management
>
> Facilities/office services staff for accommodation based changes
>
> Contractors or 3rd parties
>
> Others as applicable

Attendees at the CAB meeting may depend on the changes being considered. CAB meetings should be very focused and not waste people's time. If the CAB meeting is considered to be unproductive, then the CAB attendees will stop coming. Therefore, the meetings should be short and very focused on the changes being considered.

To accommodate multiple changes for different attendees, the CAB meetings may involve different people even during the course of a single CAB meeting. One of my clients established a morning CAB meeting that lasted for ½ hour. This ½ hour meeting was sectioned into 3 ten minute sessions. People knew when their specific changes were being discussed and would show up at the appointed session. This resulted in minimal impact to people's time and met the goals of the CAB meeting.

CAB meetings may involve suppliers, if useful. This is particularly true for a large supplier-oriented change, such as the rollout of new desktops. Other people involved in the CAB will include the Service Owner and Service Manager, the Problem Manager and the Service Level Manager.

The CAB Agenda should be published in advance of all meetings to allow the CAB members to review the proposed changes prior to the meeting. At each CAB meeting, the following agenda should be considered.

CAB Agenda

> Failed, unauthorized, backed out changes
>
> RFC's in priority order
>
> Scheduling
>
> Change reviews
>
> Change Management process
>
> Outstanding changes
>
> Advance notice of any expected RFC's

EMERGENCY CHANGES

An Emergency Change is defined as *a change that is required to be implemented in a time sensitive manner.* Emergency Changes prevent potential failure, lack or loss of functionality or lack or loss of revenue.

In a perfect world, there would be ample opportunity to ensure that all changes are evaluated, planned and implemented with proper procedures being followed. However, this is not always possible as emergencies occur that require immediate, or almost immediate, changes to be made. In such cases, emergency changes should have a path through the Change Management process and be anticipated in advance to ensure that change requirements can be met.

Authorization

Since Emergency Changes are part of the process, the process must consider these changes to provide an expedited path through the process. Authority for Emergency Changes should be delegated and documented so it can be understood.

During an Emergency Change, it may be impossible or highly inconvenient to assemble a CAB to evaluate the change. In these cases, an Emergency CAB (ECAB) may be convened. This ECAB may be a subset of the CAB and is tasked with providing as much reasonable oversight as possible during an emergency.

Testing

During an emergency, testing may not always be possible. For example, if a router fails, it is highly unlikely that a spare router is available for testing due to the cost of the extra router. In these cases, testing should be performed as much as possible, and may be done during implementation. After implementation, testing should be conducted to ensure that the change is operating as expected.

Documentation

Documentation during an Emergency Change may not always be possible to complete prior to the change occurring. However, even though it is an Emergency Change, the documentation must still be completed, but may be completed after the implementation.

Review

All Emergency Changes should be reviewed. These reviews are to determine if the change was indeed deemed to be an emergency and attempts to find ways to improve the process to reduce the numbers of Emergency Changes. Emergency Changes are inherently risky, and steps to reduce the numbers of Emergency Changes should be determined.

CHANGE POLICIES

Proper Change Management requires executive support to ensure that the Change Policies are adhered to. Executive support provides the authority to ensure that the policies are followed.

The policies that Change Management establishes must be clear, concise and decisive. While specific Change Management processes will have different policies, they should include policies for:

> Culture with zero tolerance for unauthorized changes
>
> Aligning the Change Management process with business, project and stakeholder processes
>
> Prioritization of changes
>
> Establishing accountability and responsibility
>
> Segregation of controls
>
> Establishing a single focal point for changes
>
> Removing access to people without the authority to make changes
>
> Integration to other Service Management processes
>
> Establishing change windows
>
> Performance and risk evaluation of all changes that impact service
>
> Performance measures for the Change Management process

TYPES OF CHANGE

Not all changes are created equal. Identifying change types, or classes, helps to determine the level of scrutiny that these change classes require in order to meet the requirements defined in the policies created by Change Management.

For example, adding memory to a user's desktop machine has far less impact, risk, and complexity of planning than adding memory to a server machine that supports critical business processes. Because of this disparity, these two changes should not be treated equally. Instead, these two changes should belong to different change classes with differing levels of scrutiny.

Standard Changes

Standard Changes are pre-approved changes that are well understood, common, have procedures and low risk. These types of changes are usually operational in nature and include those changes that occur within IT. Examples of these changes include changing backup schedules, submitting a batch job, or applying patches to a server.

Normal Change

Normal changes are those changes that follow the full path through the process. These types of changes undergo scrutiny and due diligence that are appropriate for the level of change. For these changes, it must be assured that appropriate planning and testing has been performed to minimize the risk associated with these changes.

Emergency Change

Emergency Changes are those that must be implemented in a time-critical manner in order to prevent unacceptable loss or impact to the business. Emergency Changes are not to be used as a mechanism because somebody needs a change quickly, but must meet specific business-impact requirements to be considered. Emergency Changes should have a path through the process and should be considered before they occur.

CHANGE MODELS

For commonly occurring changes, Change Models can be developed that pre-define the steps required to conform to the Change Management process. These Change Models are developed to pre-define the workflow, management, authorization, escalation and all other activities in change management for a particular type of change.

REMEDIATION PLANNING

Most organizations do not plan for when changes fail. Since all change has inherent risk, planning for failure must be part of that change. Remediation planning accepts the fact that a change may fail and plans for that contingency.

Explicit plans must be made for all changes in the event of failure of the change. Some remediation options include back-out planning, ensuring recovery resources are available if needed (such as having people on-call to respond to failures), and in extreme circumstances, invoking the IT Service Continuity Management plan.

Combined with Change Models, Remediation Planning only needs to be done once for each Change Model. By doing this, any change that conforms to that Change Model will have Remediation Planning already completed.

CHANGE DOCUMENTATION

All changes must be properly documented. Some changes may require more documentation than others, based on the type of change and the Change Model being used. Not all of the documentation will be available during the submission of the RFC for the change. The change documentation is completed as the change is being performed and the knowledge required for the documentation is gained.

Not all change types will require the same amount of documentation. Standard Changes require far less documentation than high-impact changes do. It is important to ensure that the amount of documentation required for a change is consistent with the type of change. Otherwise, the process is deemed too bureaucratic and will not be followed.

OVERALL ACTIVITIES

While the Change Management process has discrete activities, there are some overall activities that should be considered. These activities involve ensuring that a change is well planned, coordinated, and communicated. Communication is a key component of Change Management and involves ensuring that all stakeholders are aware of the changes before they occur and communicated after they are completed.

The overall activities include:

Planning and control of changes

Change and release scheduling

Communications

Change decision making and change authorization

Remediation planning

Measurement and control

Management reporting

Impact assessment

Continual improvement of the process

Process Activities

The diagram above shows the overall Change Management process. These activities are shown sequentially, but are often iterative. Additionally, not every type of change follows the same path through the Change Management process based on the type of change or the Change Model identified for that change.

The individual activities for the Change Management process are discussed in the following pages.

Create and Record RFC

The first activity in Change Management is to ensure that the Request for Change (RFC) has been created and that the RFC accurately reflects the change that is being proposed. An RFC is more than just a request, but often serves as an artifact that the change has occurred. This RFC documents the change, when it occurred, what the outcome was, and is a historical record of that change.

The RFC is used after the change by the Service Desk and Incident Management as a possible cause for incidents that have occurred.

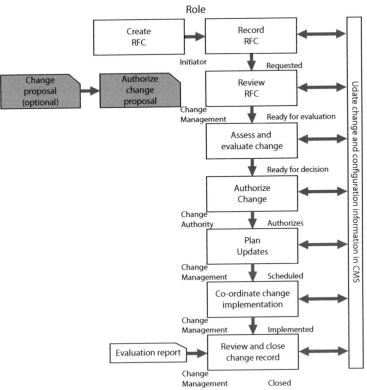

©Crown copyright 2007 - Reproduced under license from OGC

Figure 29 - Change Management Activities

Review RFC

When a change is submitted, it is reviewed to ensure that the change is correct and feasible. The correctness of the RFC assists in establishing the routing of the change to ensure that the change can be implemented in a timely manner. This is also an opportunity to reject changes that make little business sense or lack correct documentation.

Assess and Evaluate

The Assess and Evaluate activity establishes the appropriate level of change authority and ensures that the change has the appropriate level of oversight. The scope of a change is determined to identify the stakeholders of the change. These stakeholders are candidates for the Change Advisory Board (CAB).

This activity also involves assessing and evaluating the business justification, impact, cost, benefits and risk to ensure that the value of the change is worth the cost and effort. An independent evaluation of the change may be performed if required.

Service Asset and Configuration Management is consulted during the assessment as the Configuration Management System (CMS) contains details about the environment that assist with the assessment of impact and risk.

Authorize Change

Change authorization ensures that the change is understood, properly documented and is approved by all stakeholders identified for this change. Some changes may require going to a Change Advisory Board (CAB), while others may obtain approval from a single individual or may already be pre-approved according to the type of change, or associated Change Model.

Plan Updates

Planning updates involves ensuring that the change is properly planned and all change prerequisites have been completed prior to the change being implemented. Some changes require more detailed planning than others so the planning should be consistent with the scope and effort of the change.

Coordinate Change

Change Management coordinates the implementation performed by the Technical Management group, the Operations Management group or other groups. Change Management coordinates activities involved in implementing the change, but relies on functions to build, test and implement the change. These functions are discussed in Service Operation Functions.

Review and Close

Once the change has been completed, the change is reviewed for correctness and reviewed to ensure that the change met its objectives. It is also an opportunity to ensure that all documentation has been completed and saved to serve as a record of that change being performed.

A new baseline of the environment may be established that considers the new change. This baseline serves as a point to compare against the future state.

Change Reviews should occur for both successful changes and failed changes, as deemed appropriate. In particular, a failed change is not an opportunity to "point fingers," but an opportunity to improve the Change Management process. Most failed changes are usually the result of a fault in the process or a failure in adhering to the process. This review provides an opportunity to understand where these improvements can be made.

Once all actions have been completed and the documentation reviewed, the change is formally closed.

Change Management has dependencies on other processes and some optional activities. The following activities show these relationships and alternate additional activities depending on the complexity or scope of the change.

Change Proposal

Some changes may have significant complexity or cost associated with it to require a change proposal. A change proposal is submitted for those changes where the work to prepare the change or obtain funds for the change must be authorized and approved.

Authorize Proposal

When a change proposal is required, the proposal is authorized or rejected. The proposal must be authorized in order for the resources to be expended to move the change forward.

Update CMS

Upon the implementation of the change, the Configuration Management System (CMS) is updated to ensure that the CMS reflects the new state of the environment.

Evaluation Report

Upon closure of a change, the change is evaluated for correctness. This evaluation consists of an audit to ensure that the process has been adhered to. Post Implementation Reviews (PIR's) may be conducted to review complex changes and failed changes. Every Emergency Change should have a PIR to ensure that it has the appropriate oversight, even after the fact, and that it actually required an Emergency Change.

KEY PERFORMANCE INDICATORS

Change Management Key Performance Indicators (KPI's), or metrics, measure the effectiveness and the efficiency of the Change Management process. The metrics are used by the Continual Service Lifecycle stage to identify areas of improvement.

Specific metrics include:

> Number of changes implemented by service
>
> Quantifiable benefits of change
>
> Reduction in the number of disruptions
>
> Reduction in the number of unauthorized changes
>
> Reduction in the backlog of change requests
>
> Number of unplanned and emergency changes
>
> Change success rate
>
> Number of failed changes
>
> Average time to implement a change based on change type, urgency or priority
>
> Incidents attributable to changes
>
> Percentage accuracy in change estimates

ROLES

The main role for Change Management is the Change Manager. The Change Manager is responsible for all of the activities in the Change Management process and chairs the Change Advisory Board. The Change Manager ensures that all changes are properly proposed, planned, tested and implemented and that reviews are conducted for changes.

SERVICE ASSET AND CONFIGURATION MANAGEMENT

OVERVIEW

Service Asset and Configuration Management is the process that provides control to the infrastructure. Through the creation of a Configuration Model, the relationships between components are recorded to ensure that the environment is documented and well-understood. Through the documentation of the components and their relationships to each other to provide services, the service can be better supported.

The Service Asset and Configuration Management process provides the foundation for all other processes. All other processes rely on the Configuration Management System (CMS) as a repository of information regarding the environment in order to be as efficient and effective as possible.

PURPOSE

The overriding purpose of Service Asset and Configuration Management is to provide a logical model of the IT infrastructure that details all components which make up a service, along with information for each component. This is accomplished through a Configuration Management System (CMS) that stores relevant configuration and asset information, as well as relationships to each other.

Other purposes include:

Identification, controlling, recording, reporting, auditing and verifying service assets and configuration items

Accounting for, managing and protecting the integrity of these assets and configuration items through the Service Lifecycle to ensure that:

Only authorized components are use

Only authorized changes are made

Ensuring the integrity of the assets and configurations required to control the services and IT infrastructure through the Configuration Management System

Through this CMS, Configuration Management provides a central point for information to support all other Service Management processes, as well as other organizational process, such as Finance and Procurement processes.

KEY CONCEPTS

CONFIGURATION MODEL

The Service Asset and Configuration Management process includes the concept of a Configuration Model in the CMS to provide a logical model of the services in the environment. The CMS records this model for use by the other processes. This model shows the services and how the individual components, systems, and applications are related to provide these services.

Service

Services are the top level of the configuration model and should be linked to the business service that the service supports. This service should also be related to a service in the Service Catalog.

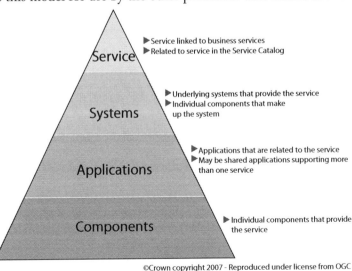

©Crown copyright 2007 - Reproduced under license from OGC

Figure 30 - Configuration Model

Systems

The systems level represents the systems that provide the service and are decomposed into the applications and components that make up this system level to support the service.

Applications

Applications are not services themselves. Applications may support one or more services, but play a role in providing the service.

Components

The component level represents the individual components, hardware, software, etc. used to provide the overall service.

Configuration models are used to model services and their underlying components within the CMS. The CMS and these configuration models are used by all other processes to provide information that makes these processes more effective and efficient. Some examples of this include:

> To assess the impact and cause of incidents and problems
>
> To assess the impact of proposed changes
>
> To plan and design new or changed services
>
> To plan technology refresh and software upgrades
>
> To plan release and deployment packages and migrate service assets to different locations and service centers
>
> To optimize asset utilization and costs

CONFIGURATION MANAGEMENT SYSTEM

The Configuration Management System (CMS) is the database that stores records of component details. This database does not have to be a single database, but could be a collection of data sources that are accessed from one place. The records stored are Configuration Items (CI's) that contain component details, as well as their relationships to each other. These records include:

> Relationships between CI's

Related incidents

Related problems

Related Known Errors

Related Change records

Release documentation

The CMS is the repository for all information related to the infrastructure and the the components that support the services. This information should be stored and related to enable quick access to it when it is needed.

CONFIGURATION ITEM

A Configuration Item (CI) is any asset, service component, or other item that is, or will be, under the control of Configuration Management. These CIs are the individual components that make up a service. In order to be a CI, it must be needed to deliver a service, be uniquely identifiable, subject to change, and can be managed. These CIs are categorized by the type of CI. Each CI also has attributes that describes information about the CI in the CMS.

Examples of CIs include the hardware and software, applications, network infrastructure, contracts, and even people. Anything could potentially be a CI if it is required to provide a service.

Each CI has a set of attributes that hold characteristics about the CI including, but not limited to, the CI name, version, model number, status, and relationships. These relationships to other CI's may include relationships to other physical components, contracts, Incidents, Problems, Changes, errors and documentation, as well as other relevant links.

CIs have a lifecycle status that shows where they are in their individual life. CIs start with a status of "on order" and move through the lifecycle (delivered, test, production, retired, etc.) until they are formally disposed.

CONFIGURATION BASELINES

Within the CMS, baselines or snapshots can be created and stored for comparative purposes against some future state. This is useful for evaluating releases for completeness, project planning, as a place to restore to if things fail, and as a blue print of the environment to duplicate in the event of a disaster.

Configuration baselines are a formally reviewed and agreed upon configuration of a service, product or infrastructure. Through these baselines, an organization can recover the infrastructure back to a specific baseline, mark a milestone in the development of a service, or perform a configuration audit. Configuration baselines are also very useful to other processes in order to prepare for disaster recovery, make changes to the infrastructure or plan for improvements.

ROLES

Configuration Management involves several roles, often performed by different people to ensure that the technology required to record the environment is well maintained, the process is effective and the media properly recorded. Other roles involve other processes to ensure that the relationships between Asset and Configuration Management and these other processes are maintained.

These roles include the following:

Service Asset Manager

The Service Asset Manager manages the Asset Management process to ensure conformance to the process and ensure that assets are identified, labeled and tracked.

Configuration Manager

The Configuration Manager ensures the Configuration Management processes is adhered to and implements the Configuration Management policy and standards.

Configuration Analyst

The Configuration Analyst supports the Configuration Management plan by ensuring accuracy of information in the CMS, performing configuration audits and providing information across the organization.

Configuration Administrator/Librarian

The Configuration Administrator/Librarian controls the receipts, identification, storage and withdrawal of all CI's in the CMS and DML, and provides information regarding these CI's. The Configuration Administrator/Librarian also maintains the Definitive Media Library (DML) and the Definitive Spares (DS).

CMS/Tools Administrator

The CMS/Tools Administrator is responsible for evaluating and maintaining the tools used in Service Asset and Configuration Management. The CMS/Tools Administrator also monitors the capacity of the CMS and ensures the integrity and performance of the Configuration Management System.

Release and Deployment Management

Overview

The transition of a service into operation is inherently risky. Many IT organizations fail to consider all of the aspects involved in the transition of a service into operations. Many times, the transition of a service involves only the installation of an application, after which, the transition team considers the transition complete and disengages from the transition. This leaves the responsibility of the service entirely to the operational staff – often without the proper training, support from second level IT and little knowledge regarding the service.

Release and Deployment Management strives to minimize the risk associated with transitioning of a service by considering all aspects of a service to ensure that the service meets the needs of the business and can be well supported. This transition involves assuring that high quality services and components are released, as well as ensuring that all elements of the release, including training, knowledge, support processes, contracts and other items are included as part of the release.

Release and Deployment Management also ensures that the service is not "installed and forgotten." Through Early Life Support, Release and Deployment Management provides resources to ensure that the service's critical early life is well supported until operations staff can fully support the service.

Purpose

Release Management's overriding purpose is to take a holistic view of a set of changes to a service and ensure that all aspects of a release, both technical and non-technical, are considered, planned, and prepared for that release. A release is far more than just the technology being provided, but also the documentation, the supporting processes and the knowledge to enable ongoing operation and continual improvement of the release after it is in operation.

The specific purposes of Release Management include:

> Defining and agreeing on release and deployment plans
>
> Ensuring that each release package consists of a set of related assets and service components that are compatible
>
> Ensuring the integrity of releases in the CMS
>
> Ensuring that all releases and deployment packages can be tracked, installed, tested, verified, uninstalled, and backed out
>
> Ensuring that organizational and stakeholder expectations are managed
>
> Recording and managing deviations, risks, and issues related to the new or changed service and take corrective action
>
> Ensuring that skills and knowledge are transferred to operations and support staff to deliver required utility and warranty

KEY CONCEPTS

Releases are usually contained in Release Packages. The definition of a Release Package is defined as *a set of Release Units that are normally distributed together*. A Release Unit is defined as *the portions of the IT infrastructure that are normally released together*.

For example, Microsoft Office is considered a Release Package. The Microsoft Office package includes many Release Units such as Microsoft Word, Microsoft Excel and Microsoft PowerPoint.

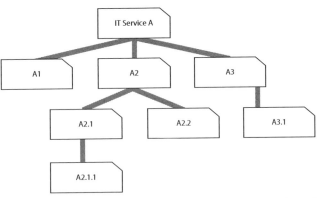

Figure 31 - Release Units and Release Packages

RELEASE OPTIONS AND CONSIDERATIONS

There are many considerations regarding releases and deployment of releases into the live environment. The three main considerations are big bang versus phased, push versus pull and automated versus manual.

Big Bang versus Phased

A big bang approach to a release is where the entire service is released into the environment at the same time. A phased release is staging a release such that the release is introduced into the live environment in a series of stages, each stage building on the previous stage.

Push versus Pull

Pushing a release into service applies the release into the environment from a central location for all users regardless of whether or not the users want the release. A pull mechanism makes the release available for users and gives the users control of when they want to install the release on their system. Popular internet messaging software and music software follow the pull model. They inform you of when a new release is available and provide you the mechanisms to install the release on your computer.

Automation versus Manual

Automated releases apply the release through automation tools. These automation tools involve software distribution tools to install the release. Automation helps to eliminate human error and makes the release repeatable. Manual releases apply the release by hand. Manual releases are usually quicker to deploy but are difficult to make repeatable and consistent.

ACTIVITIES

Release and Deployment Management activities work together to ensure that a release is properly built, packaged and tested prior to being deployed in the production environment.

Once the service package or release has been acquired from the implementation team, it

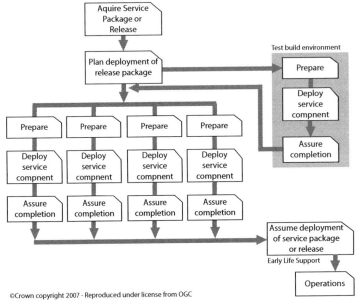

Figure 32 - Release and Deployment Management Activities

must be built and packaged in a manner that ensures consistency across the deployment environments. Once built and packaged, the release is deployed to a test environment to ensure that it can be deployed correctly.

Once the release has been deployment tested, it is deployed into the production environment(s), which may involve more than a single deployment. After deployment to the production environment, the release enters Early Life Support and is supported by both Service Transition and Service Operation until Service Operation can fully support the release.

ROLES

RELEASE AND DEPLOYMENT MANAGER

The Release and Deployment Manager ensures the policies created for release and deployment are followed to ensure management of all aspects of the end-to-end process.

The specific responsibilities of the Release and Deployment Manager are:

Update the Service Knowledge Management System (SKMS) and the Configuration Management System (CMS)

Ensures transfer of knowledge and continued control of the infrastructure

Ensures coordination of build and test

Provide management reports

Plan service roll-outs

Communication, preparation and training

Auditing hardware and software before and after a release

Ensures that the expected roll-out environment is valid and that the release affects only what it was expected to affect

RELEASE PACKAGING AND BUILD MANAGER

The Release Packaging and Build Manager is responsible for ensuring that a specific release is built and packaged correctly and finalizes the final release configuration to be deployed to the production environment. The Release Packaging and Build Manager is also responsible for reporting any outstanding known errors and workarounds to Problem Management for inclusion in the Known Error Database.

DEPLOYMENT MANAGER

The Deployment Manager ensures that the release is deployed to the production environment effectively and correctly. The Deployment Manager also assumes the responsibility for Early Life Support to ensure that the release is supported properly until Service Operation can fully assume the support responsibility for the release.

Knowledge Management

Overview

Knowledge Management is the process that ensures that organizational knowledge is stored and retained for use in Service Operation. This organizational knowledge plays a key role in not only improving the stability and supportability of a service in Service Operation, but also supporting the other Service Lifecycle stages.

Purpose

The purpose of Knowledge Management is to ensure that the right information is delivered to the appropriate place or competent person at the right time to enable informed decisions.

Knowledge Management is about retaining knowledge. Organizational knowledge begins as data. Data is discrete facts about events. Data is converted to information when we analyze the data in some context. Information with experiences, ideas, insights, values and judgment of people is called knowledge. This knowledge, along with discernment of the material and having the application and contextual awareness, is judgment.

KEY CONCEPTS

KNOWLEDGE SPIRAL/D-I-K-W MODEL

Knowledge Management strives to convert data to information to support knowledge which, in turn, can be wisely used. The intent of the Knowledge Spiral is to improve organizational knowledge by collecting data, distilling information from it, obtaining knowledge from the information that facilitates wisdom. Data, Information, Knowledge and Wisdom are not synonymous. The Knowledge Spiral is also known as the D-I-K-W Model.

Data is defined as *numbers, characters, images or other outputs from devices to convert physical quantities into symbols. Data is quantitative.*

Information is defined as *a message received and understood. Information is a collection of facts from which a conclusion can be drawn.*

Knowledge is defined as *information combined with the experience, context, interpretation and reflection.*

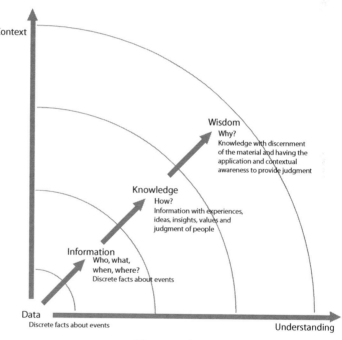

Figure 33 - Data-Information-Knowledge-Wisdom Model

Wisdom is defined as *the ability to make correct judgments and decisions.*

Data, Information, and Knowledge can be stored for later use through the Service Management Knowledge System (SKMS). Wisdom however, cannot be retained as wisdom is the ability to make correct decisions based on this knowledge.

ACTIVITIES

The activities in Knowledge Management are focused on understanding the sources of knowledge and developing techniques to retain this knowledge. These activities include:

Knowledge Management Strategy

Developing a Knowledge Management strategy involves understanding what knowledge to capture, deciding where and when the knowledge will be captured, and deciding who will capture the knowledge. This strategy should consider all stages of the Service Lifecycle as critical knowledge is inherent within all stages.

Knowledge Transfer

Knowledge Transfer involves sharing knowledge between parts of the organization. When developing processes, particularly those that involve transfer of responsibilities for services, the knowledge should be focused on, as well. Specific points in the process should be determined when knowledge will be transferred from one part of the organization to another.

Data and Information Management

This activity involves development and maintenance of the Service Knowledge Management System (SKMS). The SKMS is a system in which organizational knowledge is captured, maintained and available for use by others in the organization.

Using the SKMS

Using the SKMS involves understanding what knowledge is useful, how it will be used, and how it will be accessed. This activity involves understanding the consumers of the knowledge to develop a system that will be useful, accessible, and contain pertinent knowledge.

CHAPTER REVIEW

Service Transition Processes

>Change Management
>
>Release and Deployment Management
>
>Service Asset and Configuration Management
>
>Knowledge Management

Change Management

Purpose

>To ensure that standardized methods and procedures are used for efficient and prompt handling of all changes

7 R's of Change Management

>Who RAISED the change?
>
>What is the REASON for the change?
>
>What is the RETURN required from the change?
>
>What are the RISKS involved in the change?
>
>What RESOURCES are required to deliver the change?
>
>Who is RESPONSIBLE for the build, test, and implementation of the change?
>
>What is the RELATIONSHIP between this change and other changes?

Change Priority

>The priority is based on the urgency and impact.

Change Advisory Board

>Name provided for the group of stakeholders that meet to evaluate high impact requests for change

Emergency Change

A change that is required to be implemented in a time sensitive manner

Types of Change

Standard Changes
Normal Change
Emergency Change

Activities

Change Proposal (optional)
Create and Record RFC
Review RFC
Assess and Evaluate
Authorize Change
Plan Updates
Coordinate Change
Review and Close
Update CMS
Evaluation Report

Roles

Change Manager

Responsible for all of the activities in the Change Management process and chairs the Change Advisory Board.

Service Asset and Configuration Management

Purpose

To provide a logical model of the IT infrastructure that details all components which make up a service, along with information for each component

Configuration Management System (CMS)

Database that stores records of component details

Configuration Item (CI)

Any asset, service component, or other item that is, or will be, under the control of Configuration Management

Roles

Service Asset Manager

Manages the Asset Management process to ensure conformance to the process and ensure that assets are identified, labeled and tracked

Configuration Manager

Ensures the Configuration Management processes is adhered to and implements the Configuration Management policy and standards.

Configuration Analyst

Supports the Configuration Management plan by ensuring accuracy of information in the CMS, performing configuration audits and providing information across the organization.

Configuration Administrator/Librarian

Controls the receipts, identification, storage and withdrawal of all CI's in the CMS and DMS, and provides information regarding these CI's

CMS/Tools Administrator

Responsible for evaluating and maintaining the tools used in Service Asset and Configuration Management

Release and Deployment Management

Purpose

To take a holistic view of a set of changes to a service and ensure that all aspects of a release, both technical and non-technical, are considered, planned, and prepared for that release

Definitions

Release Unit   The portions of the IT infrastructure that are normally released together

Release Package   A set of Release Units that are normally distributed together

Release Options and Considerations

Big Bang versus Phased

Push versus Pull

Automation versus Manual

Roles

Release and Deployment Manager

Ensures the policies created for release and deployment are followed to ensure management of all aspects of the end-to-end process.

Release Packaging and Build Manager

Responsible for ensuring that a specific release is built and packaged correctly and finalizes the final release configuration to be deployed to the production environment.

Deployment Manager

Ensures that the release is deployed to the production environment effectively and correctly

Knowledge Management

Purpose

The purpose of Knowledge Management is to ensure that the right information is delivered to the appropriate place or competent person at the right time to enable informed decisions

Definitions

Data	Numbers, characters, images or other outputs from devices to convert physical quantities into symbols. Data is quantitative.
Information	A message received and understood. Information is a collection of facts from which a conclusion can be drawn
Knowledge	Information combined with the experience, context, interpretation and reflection
Wisdom	The ability to make correct judgments and decision

Knowledge Spiral/D-I-K-W Model

Improve organizational knowledge by collecting data, distilling information from it, obtaining knowledge from the information that facilitates wisdom.

CHAPTER QUIZ

1. The Service Transition processes include:

    a. Change Management

    b. Service Asset and Configuration Management

    c. Release and Deployment Management

    d. Knowledge Management

    e. Problem Management

2. Which process ensures that standardized methods and procedures are used for efficient and prompt handling of all changes?

    a. Change Management

    b. Release and Deployment Management

    c. Knowledge Management

    d. Service Asset and Configuration Management

3. The 7 R's of Change Management include:

    a. Raised

    b. Return

    c. Resources

    d. Relationship

    e. Review

    f. Reason

    g. Risks

    h. Responsible

    i. Rating

4. All changes should be treated the same regardless of complexity, scope or risk.

    a. True
    b. False

5. Match the type of change with its characteristic.

    a. Must be done to prevent loss of business revenue
    b. Pre-approved
    c. Regular Change

    i.   Normal Change
    ii.   Standard Change
    iii. Emergency Change

6. What is the term used for the explicit plans that are made for all changes in the event of a change failure?

    a. IT Service Continuity Management
    b. Remediation Planning
    c. Back out Planning
    d. Post Implementation Review

7. Change Models should include pre-defined timescales and what other items(s)?

    a. Authorization levels
    b. Escalation procedures
    c. Responsibilities
    d. Reporting requirements

8.   All changes require a change proposal.

  a.   True
  b.   False

9.   Priority of a change, incident, or problem is determined by what?

  a.   Impact and Business Schedule
  b.   Resource Availability and Impact
  c.   Urgency and Impact
  d.   Business Schedule and Operational Schedule

10.   The CAB is responsible for what?

  a.   Evaluating high-impact requests for change
  b.   Performing a Post Implementation Review of all changes
  c.   Evaluating all requests for change
  d.   Informing the business of impending outages to implement changes

11.   Emergency changes have no place in Change Management.

  a.   True
  b.   False

12.   Emergency Changes should only be used to prevent:

  a.   The requestor from complaining
  b.   Access to a Service Request
  c.   All potential failures
  d.   Lack or loss of revenue

13. Before an Emergency Change is implemented, the CAB must be convened.

   a. True
   b. False

14. What is the name of the process that provides a logical model of the IT infrastructure and holds its data in the CMS?

   a. Service Modeling
   b. Service Asset and Configuration Management
   c. Release and Deployment Management
   d. Demand Management

15. What are the characteristics of a Configuration Item (CI)?

   a. Needed to deliver a service
   b. Is highly valuable and depreciated each fiscal year
   c. Uniquely identifiable
   d. Can be managed
   e. Subject to change

16. What types of information might be stored as a CI in the CMS?

   a. Known Errors
   b. Incidents
   c. Serial Number
   d. Problems
   e. Change Records
   f. Quantity on Hand
   g. Release Documentation

17.   What is the name given for the place where definitive versions of software are stored?

   a.   Federated Database
   b.   Definitive Media Library
   c.   Definitive Software Library
   d.   Software Catalog

18.   Release and Deployment Management has many purposes. What are three of these from the list below?

   a.   Ensure that a release is properly coded and all code is managed in the CMS
   b.   Ensure that organization and stakeholder change is managed
   c.   Ensure the integrity of a release in the CMS
   d.   Ensure that skills and knowledge are transferred to operation

19.   What is a Release Unit?

   a.   A tested unit of code
   b.   All of the hardware and software that make up a service
   c.   A set of packages that are installed to support a service
   d.   The portions of the IT infrastructure that are normally released together

20.   A Package is defined as a set of Release Units that are normally distributed together.

   a.   True
   b.   False

21.   Release Management considerations involve determining an approach to a release. Match the approach considerations.

        a.   Big Bang
        b.   Push
        c.   Automation

        i.   Phased
        ii.   Pull
        iii.   Manual

22.   Which of the following cannot be stored in a database or management system?

        a.   Knowledge
        b.   Wisdom
        c.   Data
        d.   Information

23.   What is the order of the Knowledge Spiral?

        a.   Collection->Correlation->Normalization->Analysis
        b.   Data->Knowledge->Wisdom->Information
        c.   Data->Knowledge->Information->Wisdom
        d.   Data->Information->Knowledge->Wisdom

24.   Discrete facts about events are called:

        a.   Knowledge
        b.   Wisdom
        c.   Information
        d.   Data

25. Data in context is called:

   a. Knowledge
   b. Wisdom
   c. Information
   d. Data

26. Information with experiences, ideas, insights, values and judgment of people is called:

   a. Knowledge
   b. Wisdom
   c. Information
   d. Data

27. Knowledge with discernment of the material and having the application and contextual awareness to provide judgment is called:

   a. Knowledge
   b. Wisdom
   c. Information
   d. Data

Answers

1.	A, B, C, D
2.	A
3.	A, B, C, D, F, G, H
4.	B
5.	A – iii, B – ii, C – i
6.	B
7.	A, B, C
8.	B
9.	C
10.	A
11.	B
12.	A, C, D
13.	B
14.	B
15.	A, C, D, E
16.	A, B, D, E, G
17.	B
18.	B, C, D
19.	D
20.	A
21.	A – i, B – ii, C – iii
22.	B
23.	D
24.	D
25.	C
26.	A
27.	B

SERVICE OPERATION PROCESSES

OVERVIEW

Service Operation is the stage of the Service Lifecycle where the value is delivered to the customer and it is where the strategy of the organization is executed. Within Service Operation are the processes to ensure that this value can be provided effectively and efficiency. In this section, these processes are discussed.

The processes in Service Operation are:

> Incident Management
>
> Event Management
>
> Request Fulfillment
>
> Problem Management
>
> Access Management

These processes should work closely together to ensure that the service is well supported and any requests regarding the service can be fulfilled.

Incident Management

Geppetto Garcia's

Geppetto Garcia's, just like any other publicly traded company, is required to report to the Security and Exchange Commission (SEC) each quarter by a certain date. They must submit the proper financial statements to the SEC or risk being in violation of regulatory requirements. The financial information that needs to be submitted includes their Income Statement, Cash Flow Statement and Balance Sheet.

Andrea Dawson, a financial analyst, is preparing the forms for submission to the SEC. Andrea realizes that the printer on which she is trying to print the reports is not working and won't print her reports. Andrea calls the Service Desk to report the issue.

The Service Desk, upon getting Andrea's call, asks her some questions about what it is she is trying to do. They are determining what her business desired outcomes are. Printing itself is not a critical service, but an enabling service. They quickly realize that the service being impacted is the Financial Reporting Service. According to the SLAs that the Service Desk has access to, the Financial Reporting Service is critical during this time frame to prevent violations of regulatory reporting requirements.

The Service Desk attempts to print to the printer and finds that they cannot print to the printer either. Seeing that this printer has had issues in the past, they perform a workaround and map Andrea's computer to a printer further down the hall.

Andrea tests the print and finds that printing of her reports has been fixed. Andrea prints her financial reports, gets the Chief Operating Officer's signature, and then gets them sent to the SEC where they arrive on time.

The Service Desk, after ensuring that Andrea's issue has been resolved, closes this incident.

Many people that I teach have issues with this scenario. Their main issue is the question "what about the printer?" In Incident Management, the printer is irrelevant. Incident

Management is not about fixing the underlying problem, such as the printer, but about restoring service as quickly as possible through whatever reasonable means necessary.

We will get back to the printer in the Problem Management process.

OVERVIEW

The Incident Management process objective is to restore normal service operation as quickly as possible and minimize the adverse impact on business operations, thus ensuring that the best possible levels of service quality and availability are maintained. To achieve this objective, Incident Management does not focus on fixing the underlying problem. Instead, Incident Management employs the use of workarounds to restore service as quickly as possible. This rapid restoration of service minimizes the adverse impact to business and improves customer and user satisfaction.

Incident Management is guided by the Service Level Agreements. The SLA's document the expected levels of service for response targets for Incident Management. Incident Management may also use the information in the SLA's to determine relative priorities of incidents.

The Service Desk initiates the Incident Management process based on calls received. For incidents that the Service Desk can resolve, the Service Desk handles the incident from recording to closure. For incidents that are beyond the technical ability of the Service Desk or that are too complex, other resources are utilized. Through the relationship with the Service Desk, Incident Management helps to ensure that resources are utilized in an optimal manner by using specialized staff for the incidents that cannot be managed at the Service Desk.

The Incident Management process records every incident that occurs in the environment. These incidents are tracked to ensure that no incident is lost, forgotten, or ignored. These incidents are also managed to ensure that they are responded to and resolved according to the Service Level Agreements.

PURPOSE

Incident Management ensures that service is restored as quickly as possible and the adverse impact to the business is minimized. Incident Management coordinates the activities of everyone involved in restoring service to ensure that service is restored according to the SLA's. Incident Management also ensures that no incident is lost, forgotten, or ignored.

Business Value

Incident Management is one of the most visible processes to the business. Business values the Incident Management process through the ability to detect and resolve incidents which results in lower downtime to the business which, in turn, means higher availability of the service. While the business may not notice that a service is operating better than expected, they definitely notice when the service is unavailable. Incident Management strives to reduce downtime for the benefit of the business.

Proper prioritization of incidents can provide alignment between IT and real-time business priorities. This requires that the Incident Management process has knowledge about the business processes and any changes to those processes. Much of this information is conveyed in the Service Level Agreements.

Incident Management and the Service Desk are in constant communication with the users of IT services. Because of this, Incident Management and the Service Desk are well-positioned to identify improvements required for the business, such as service improvements, additional training requirements, process improvements, etc.

Key Concepts

An incident is defined as ***an unplanned interruption to an IT service or reduction in the quality of an IT service***. Incident Management is responsible for managing these incidents to minimize impact of an incident. Incident Management is defined as the process for dealing with all incidents, including failures, questions or queries reported by the users, by technical staff, or automatically detected and reported by event monitoring tools. In essence, an incident can be reported from any source – users, technicians, monitoring tools, etc. Regardless of the source of an incident, an incident is an incident. Just because a technician reports something to the Service Desk, does not make it a problem, but an incident.

TIMESCALES

To best support the expectations of business, the Incident Management process should be well-documented with predefined timescales of each stage of the process. These timescales may be driven by the Service Level Agreements and may differ based on priority of the incident. All support groups must be made aware of these timescales to ensure that they can meet the requirements for responding to incidents.

INCIDENT MODELS

Most of the incidents that occur in an environment are not unique. Many organizations report that 80% or more of their incident volumes are incidents that they have seen before and have experience with. In these cases, Incident Models can be used to pre-define the steps required, responsibilities, timescales, escalation procedures and resolutions for these incidents. Incident Models can reduce the response time greatly by documenting the incident and the steps required to resolve it in anticipation of the incident re-occurring.

MAJOR INCIDENTS

Major Incidents are those incidents with a high level of disruption to the business. While IT Service Management strives to eliminate Major Incidents, they should be anticipated. Major Incidents should be pre-defined with an expedited path through the process for quick resolution. Major Incidents have the highest priority for resolution so when possible, these resolutions steps should be expedited.

ESCALATION

At times, the Service Desk, or anyone who is investigating an incident, may not have the ability to determine how to resolve the incident. This may require the incident to be escalated to a person or group with more specialized knowledge of that service or component. This is known as functional escalation.

An incident may also be escalated to a supervisor, manager, director, or higher in order to notify them of the incident and possible impact, as well as to obtain resources to resolve this incident. This is known as hierarchic escalation. Users can initiate hierarchic escalation to request more attention be provided for their incident.

Escalation, both functional and hierarchic, could also occur when SLA timeframes are about to expire. This escalation provides an additional mechanism to ensure that incidents can be resolved to meet the needs of the business.

ACTIVITIES

Incidents can come from anywhere in the environment. Users can call the Service Desk to report incidents or they can originate from Technical Management, IT operations Management, event monitoring tools or even vendors. While many of the incidents are initiated with the Service Desk, this is not required as other sources of incidents, such as monitoring tools, automate submission to the Incident Management process.

It is important to note that Incident Management interfaces with other processes such as Problem Management, Request Fulfillment, Event Management and Change Management. Incident Management could involve anyone within the organization. Because, depending on the nature of the incident, anyone in the

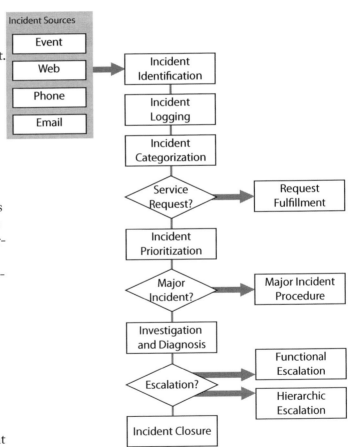

©Crown copyright 2007 - Reproduced under license from OGC

Figure 34 - Incident Management Activities

organization may be required to respond to the incident.

Identification

When an incident occurs, it is not always readily identified as an incident. Even though a service may be impacted, the Service Desk may not be notified until much later. Monitoring tools assist with the identification of an incident to reduce the time it takes to begin taking corrective action.

Logging

Every incident must be logged effectively. Logging an incident involves ensuring that all relevant documentation regarding an incident is recorded to reduce unnecessary communication. This documentation may be updated as required as more information becomes available regarding the incident.

The resulting incident records are vital to identifying trends in service and identify areas for improvement, as well as to provide information that can be referred to later to resolve other similar incidents. These records become part of the Service Knowledge Management System (SKMS) along with other records and information.

Categorization

Once the incident is logged, it is categorized according to the type of incident and what it affects. Categorization is used for correct escalation to specialist groups, reporting and incident matching. Incident matching involves researching previous incidents to see if there is a similar incident for which the resolution can be leveraged to resolve the current incident.

The Incident Management process may determine that the incident is actually a Service Request. Service Requests are managed by the Request Fulfillment process. Service Requests interact with Incident Management because the user contacts the Service Desk to report an incident or to obtain some service. The Service Desk begins the logging and categorization of the call to ensure that the information is recorded for all calls, not just incidents.

Prioritization

Incidents are prioritized based on urgency and impact. When multiple incidents occur at once, they must be prioritized in order to resolve the most important incidents before less important incidents. Urgency is defined as *the time within which the incident must be resolved in order to meet business deadlines.* This is usually determined by the user and is a subjective measure of priority. Impact, however, is the objective measure of the priority and is defined by *the likely affect that the incident will have on the business service being disrupted.* The priority may change over time as urgency, impact, or both, change.

Major Incidents, as discussed previously, have the highest priority and they should have an expedited path through the process.

Initial Diagnosis

The Service Desk provides the initial diagnosis of an incident based on their knowledge, diagnostic scripts, known errors, or other information they may have. Over time, the Service Desk's ability to perform an initial diagnosis will improve as they become more able to recognize the incident.

Investigation and Diagnosis

Investigation and diagnosis includes understanding the true nature of the event. In this activity, the incident is analyzed to understand what has occurred and the events leading up to the failure. The impact will be confirmed, which may result in updating the priority of the incident. The possible causes for the incident will be reviewed to determine the approach for resolving the incident. Note that while Incident Management is not necessarily determining the root cause of the failure, the root cause may still be uncovered. Incident Management's objective is to restore the service, not to determine the root cause. However, the root cause may still be determined and the error removed if this is the quickest path to resolution.

In this activity, previous incidents to the current one are researched to determine if this incident has occurred in the past. Called Incident Matching, any matches to incidents are reviewed to leverage any knowledge that exists in past incidents. Through proper documentation of incidents, historical incidents can be leveraged to provide swift resolution should those incidents occur again.

Resolution and Recovery

Resolution is performed when the most appropriate action is determined. The potential resolution is tested either by the resolution implementer, the user, or both. Once the incident has been resolved, recovery may be necessary to restore the service to its operational state. This may involve recovering data or recovering transactions. Upon restoration and recovery, the incident is passed back to the Service Desk for formal closure.

The incident is closed when the Service Desk verifies that the resolution satisfied the user expectations and the service has been restored. This includes determining a closure code for the incident, ensuring the incident is correctly documented and conducting a user satisfaction survey (probably through email or web).

Closure

The Service Desk performs formal closure of the incident by verifying that the user is satisfied with the resolution. The Service Desk reviews the incident record to assign a closure category, ensure the documentation is completed, and conduct a user satisfaction survey. Based on the outcome of the incident, the Service Desk may consider opening a problem record for further action.

Once an incident is closed, it may be reopened if the incident has not been fully resolved. However, rules must be established to determined how an incident can be reopened and by whom.

KEY PERFORMANCE INDICATORS

Key Performance Indicators (KPI's) for Incident Management focus on improving the Incident Management process to ensure that incidents are resolved in a timely manner and to improve responsiveness. The KPI's include:

> Total number of incidents
>
> Breakdown of incidents at each stage of the lifecycle
>
> Size of current incident backlog
>
> Number and percentage of major incidents
>
> Mean elapsed time to resolve
>
> Percentage of incidents handled within agreed response times
>
> Average cost per incident
>
> Number and percentage of incidents reopened
>
> Number and percentage of incidents incorrectly assigned

Number and percentage of incidents incorrectly categorized

Percentage of incidents closed by the Service Desk without referring to other groups

Number and percentage of incidents processed per Service Desk agent

Number and percentage of incidents resolved remotely without requiring a visit

Number of incidents handled by each incident model

Breakdown of incidents by time of day to help pinpoint peaks and ensure matching of resources

ROLES

Incident Management potentially affects everyone in the organization. Therefore, everyone plays a role in Incident Management. The specific Incident Management roles are listed below.

Incident Manager

The Incident Manager is responsible for the overall process and ensuring that the activities in the process are carried out. For most organizations, there is only one Incident Manager, but in larger, particularly multi-national organizations, there may be multiple Incident Managers to manage the process locally.

The Incident Manager is specifically responsible for ensuring the effectiveness and efficiency of the process, managing the work of 1st and 2nd level support and developing the Incident Management process and procedures. The Incident Manager oversees any Major Incidents that occur to manage them through resolution. The Incident Manager also develops the Incident Management System and provides management information to the organization.

1st Level Support

The 1st level support staff consists of the Service Desk personnel. They are responsible for the activities at the Service Desk when related to Incidents.

2nd Level Support

2nd level support staff includes personnel with greater technical skill than the Service Desk. The 2nd level support staff resolves incidents they are assigned. These incidents are usually beyond the abilities of the Service Desk or they require more time to resolve effectively.

3rd Level Support

The 3rd level support teams are internal teams and external vendors with specific knowledge required to resolve an Incident. These teams are responsible for resolving incidents for which they are assigned usually requiring specialized skill and knowledge.

CHALLENGES

Incident Management is highly visible to the business which is challenging by itself. Incident Management must overcome many challenges to ensure effectiveness and efficiency of the processes. These challenges include:

Ability to detect events as early as possible

Earlier detection improves response time. The Event Management process using monitoring tools strives to improve detection time, and take the appropriate control action for events. This control action includes initiating an incident, when appropriate.

Convincing all staff that incidents must be logged

Logging events takes time. However, it is critical to log events to ensure that records are kept as a basis on which to improve as well as justify resources.

Encouraging the use of self-help web-based capabilities

Users can resolve their incidents more quickly using self-help resources if they are available to them. However, users may require training on how to access this self-help. Some users, however, will be hesitant to use self-help and must still be managed in person.

Availability of information about problems and Known Errors

Incident Management relies heavily on information about services in order to resolve incidents effectively and efficiently. Incident Management must have access to documented problems and Known Errors.

Integration to the CMS

The Configuration Management System (CMS) provides the relationships between CI's for a service. Incident Management relies heavily on this information and the history of CI's to resolve incidents.

Integration to the SLM process

Service Level Management provides the response times for Incident Management, as well as impact and priority definitions and escalation procedures.

CRITICAL SUCCESS FACTORS

Incident Management starts at the Service Desk. The Service Desk ensures that incidents are well-managed from the first call to closure.

Without Service Level Agreements, Incident Management does not have an authoritative source of response times for incidents. Without SLA's, Incident Management provides only a best effort approach at meeting the response times of the business. SLA's must clearly define the resolution targets for Incident Management.

The Incident Management staff must have a business focus and be customer oriented. It is not enough to be technical when responding to incidents, but Incident Management must have the ability to communicate in terms the business understands while meeting their requirements.

Tools and technology are critical to Incident Management. Incidents must be recorded in a way that they can utilize later when responding to other incidents. The Incident Management System must also be integrated to other processes to ensure seamless interaction between the processes.

Lastly, Incident Management is a team effort. Operational Level Agreements (OLA's) must be established that define the relationships between support groups and their responsibilities to restore service. These OLA's must take into consideration the Service Level Agreements and be established in alignment with these SLA's. OLA's alone do not provide the proper behavior. Staff motivation to achieve the requirements in the OLA's must be managed effectively.

Risks

Without the proper training and expertise at the Service Desk, incidents will not be effectively resolved. This lack of training may result in resources becoming overwhelmed with incidents.

If the incidents are not well managed, they risk becoming bogged down and not progressing. Support tools are required to ensure that these incidents and their timeframes are managed and alerts are generated to provide notification of delays. These tools must also provide adequate information about the process overall.

If OLAs and contracts are not in place to support the process, Incident Management will not be able to resolve the incidents effectively. Without these defined responsibilities, extra effort will be expended determining where the responsibilities lie during the resolution of the incident.

Event Management

Geppetto Garcia's

Within Geppetto Garcia's infrastructure, events are flowing on a regular basis. Events communicate things that occur in their environment such as submission of a meal order, a customer payment transaction has occurred, someone logged into a server, a batch job has started, etc. These events occur all the time and in such frequency that there is no potential way that a human can discern what these events mean.

Some events are benign, while other events suggest something out of the ordinary. Combinations of events, such as someone attempting to log into a server multiple times with the wrong password, may be indicative of something out of the ordinary. To detect these events and determine if any action should be taken, Geppetto Garcia's has employed the use of an Event Management tool to detect these events, correlate the events and take the appropriate control action.

Many times, this Event Management tool has detected issues in the environment before the user was impacted. On one occasion, it was detected that the drive capacity on a key database server was about to fill up. If this database server had been impacted, Geppetto Garcia's inventory control service may have been disrupted. If the inventory control service is disrupted, then food and supplies may not be ordered in time for individual restaurants resulting in meals not being available for diners.

By the quick detection of this event, the Event Management tool automatically cleaned the drive to get rid of temporary files and compressed the databases. This automated action, as well as notification of the event, prevented an outage and provided important information to Capacity Management to analyze the capacity requirements for this server.

OVERVIEW

Event Management provides the ability to detect events, make sense of them and determine that the appropriate control action is provided. Event Management is the basis for Operational Management and control, and is used for automating Operations Management activities.

In today's IT organization, events occur on a regular basis. Many of these events are used as a mechanism for communication between devices to perform actions such as start scripts, creating user accounts, and many other activities. Some of these events, however, require some form of action or intervention such as incidents. Other events cause triggers for certain Service Management processes to initiate some action. A major incident, for example, would initiate some action from Availability Management and Service Level Management to review the outage and determine a resolution.

An Event is defined *as any detectable or discernible occurrence that has significance for the management of the IT infrastructure or the delivery of IT service and evaluation of the impact a deviation might cause to the services*. Note that an event is significant to the service, not necessarily to us. Significant events to the service include notification of batch jobs starting and stopping, someone logging into a server, a transaction occurred, among others. It is up to Event Management to determine when these are significant to us and let us know.

KEY CONCEPTS

EVENT TYPES

There can be of many types of events. Some events reflect a normal situation or initiate some action, such as starting a batch job, while others signify an abnormal situation, such as an outage or a batch job failing to run.

Regular Operation

Events occur in the environment all the time. Most applications, computers, and network devices are instrumented with events that inform other components of activities. These types of events signify regular operation, such as a user logging on to a computer or a batch job that has been completed.

Exceptional

Exceptional events are those that signify something out of the ordinary occurring. For example, when a user attempts a login with an invalid password, a threshold on a computer has been violated, or a PC scan reveals unauthorized software, an exception event may be generated.

Many times these events may generate an alert. An alert is a form of communication that brings this event to the attention of someone or something to consider taking action.

Unusual, but not Exceptional

Unusual events are types of exceptional events that signify unusual, but not exceptional activities. For example, a batch job may be taking longer than normal or a threshold has almost been violated.

ACTIVITIES

Events can come from a number of different sources. Hardware and software can be instrumented to communicate events. Most of these events are notifications or informal, but Event Management must try to make sense of the events and take action when it is required.

Understanding what all these events mean requires knowledge and involvement from throughout the organization. This knowledge is used to design instrumentation to generate the events, design filtering criteria to understand what events are important, developing correlation rules that evaluate combinations of events and how they may be related, and developing automatic and human responses to events.

Event Detection

When events are initiated, they are useless unless they are detected. Detection depends largely on the technology being utilized to monitor these events.

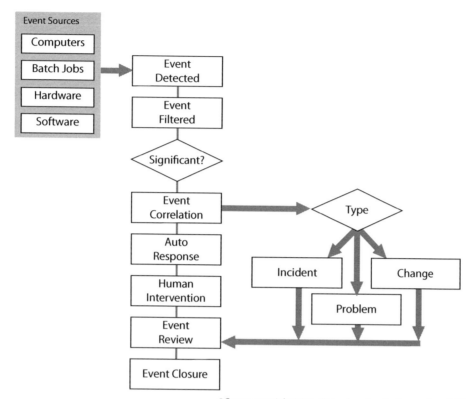

Figure 35 - Event Management Activities

Event Filtering

Once detected, the events are filtered to determine the significance. Not all events require any action, so the filtering activity suppresses these events to prevent the Event Management process from being overwhelmed with events. This filtering determines the significance of the event.

Significance

The significance of the event is determined by the categorization of the event. Event levels are then applied to events to determine what actions to take based on the event. These event levels may include:

Informational

Informational events do not require a response

Warning

Warning events refer to events that approach a threshold or when a redundant device fails

Exception

An exception event represents something in the environment that has failed. Many times, but not always, these events initiate an incident that is opened in Incident Management.

Event Correlation

Events can come from a variety of sources and a determination is required to see if these events may be related in some way. Event correlation uses correlation rules to make the determination if events are related. If events are related, then a new event may be created to make Event Management aware of this relationship. Correlation may also modify a specific event based on its correlation rules. For example, if the same event occurs multiple times in a short time period, the correlation may determine that the series of events is more significant than if only one event were to occur in that same time period.

If the event is significant, as determined through correlation, the event will be typed into an Incident, Problem or Change. Other types may also apply depending on your process.

Review Actions

If actions are required for an event, the actions are reviewed prior to closure.

Close Event

Most events do not have a status like incidents or problems, but they simply exist. The closure of an event is linked to the incident, problem, or change that is created as a result of an event.

Response Selection

When determining a response to an event, there are several options available. These options include:

Event Logging

All events should be logged in some manner in case they need to be referred to or audited later.

Automatic Response

Some events have automatic actions designed into the Event Management System.

Problem Management assists in determining these automatic responses, as well as Service Design establishing automatic responses during the design of the service.

Alerts and Human Intervention

When events require a specific action, an alert is generated to trigger this action. This action may require human intervention.

Incident

When opening an incident, any existing diagnostic information should be included to speed incident resolution.

Problem

Multiple incidents may require opening a Problem Record for evaluation.

Change

Changes may be opened based on an event signifying that a threshold has been violated. The correlation engine specifies the conditions for which the change should be opened.

Not all events require handling of this nature. For example, when a redundant CI has failed, notification of the event should be performed, but it doesn't require an immediate response.

Roles

Event Management is performed by existing roles in the environment. These roles include activities in the Service Operation stage, as well as the Service Design and Service Transition stage of the Service Lifecycle. These roles include the Service Desk, Technical Management, Applications Management and IT Operations Management.

Service Desk

The Service Desk responds to events. Usually, these events are filtered through IT Operations Management before the Service Desk is notified.

Technical and Applications Management

The Technical and Applications Management functions resolve the related incidents and problems to events. They also train the Service Desk and IT Operations functions the appropriate response actions to take for specific events.

In Service Design, these functions design events into a service, including instrumentation, classification and automatic responses to events. These functions also determine the relationships between events to populate the correlation engine with the appropriate responses.

In Service Transition, these functions are responsible for testing the events and ensuring that the designed responses are tested and appropriate for operational control of the service.

IT Operations Management

IT Operations Management has primary responsibility for monitoring the events to ensure the availability of services.

REQUEST FULFILLMENT

GEPPETTO GARCIA'S

In order to facilitate the needs of the business, Mark Renner recognized that not all calls into the Service Desk are incidents. Based upon historical records, Mark realized that about half of the calls into the Service Desk are not regarding disruption to business. Instead, these calls are about requests for something to be done for the user.

Based on this information, and the published Service Catalog, Mark established a Request Fulfillment process with the Service Desk. This Request Fulfillment process provides a mechanism for requests based on the Service Catalog, to be fulfilled. Mark has integrated the Service Catalog with the Service Desk to provide a web-based front end for many types of contact with the Service Desk.

The Request Fulfillment process has helped the Service Desk prioritize on what is important. Through analysis of the requests, many of the requests have now been automated providing users access to self-help Service Desk capabilities. Based on the most common types of requests, the Service Desk found that the most common and labor-intensive request is installation of new user software. As a result, the Service Desk implemented self-help capabilities that provide users access to software to be installed on demand. This access to back end processes and reducing the interaction of Service Desk staff has resulted in the Service Desk being far more responsive to incidents and improving the productivity of the user community.

OVERVIEW

A Service Request is defined as a request for a change to be made to a service that is usually requested by the user, is low risk, low impact, common and recurrent. These requests are those requests that occur on a regular basis, such as adding software to a computer, requesting an office move, or requesting a cell phone or pager along with many other types of requests. Most Service Requests are based on services in the Service Catalog.

Purpose

Request Fulfillment is the process that is responsible for managing requests from users to ensure that they are addressed in a timely manner according to the organization's policies. Other objectives of Request Fulfillment include:

> Providing a channel for users to request and receive standard services for which a pre-defined approval and qualification process exists
>
> Providing information to users and customers about the availability of services and the procedure for obtaining them
>
> Sourcing and delivering the components of requested standard services
>
> Assisting with the general information, complaints or comments regarding services

Key Concepts

Users regularly request many types of services. Most, if not all, service requests are initiated due to a published product or service present in the Service Catalog. With an online Service Catalog, many service requests can be initiated within the Service Catalog, similar to an online shopping experience.

Requested services can be supplied through internal or external support teams. Adding software, for example, is usually provided through internal support teams through software distribution tools. A cell phone or pager request is also provided through internal support teams but using external providers for equipment, service contracts and fee schedules.

Requests are not always automatic. Some requests may require approval to ensure that the requestor is entitled to receive the service. Funding may also be required to obtain the components to fulfill the request. This funding may also require approval.

Request Models are similar to Incident Models. Request Models are established to automate responses to commonly occurring requests. These models can automate the workflow in fulfilling the request, as well as document the fulfillment activities.

ROLES

A Service Request is handled similarly to incidents. The Service Desk has first line responsibility to respond to service requests. Service requests are handled using existing teams, such as the Service Desk and other functional teams. The procurement department may also be involved, particularly when a request involves purchasing new equipment.

A service request may involve other teams outside of IT. An example of this could be a request to onboard a new employee. To service this request, it would require the involvement of not only IT for computer equipment and networking, but also HR, office coordination, telephony services and, perhaps, other teams.

PROBLEM MANAGEMENT

GEPPETTO GARCIA'S

Mark Renner noticed that the IT organization was very reactive. It seemed that everyone in IT was responding to incidents in the environment. This caused IT to become overwhelmed, forcing the organization to work nights and weekends, and the quality and timeliness of projects was declining. Mark realized that he needed to find a way to reduce the reactive nature of the IT organization and make it more proactive. One way he found to do this is by reducing the number of incidents that occurred in the environment. To address this, Mark turned to Problem Management.

Mark began by analyzing the incident history. He quickly realized that there were incidents that were occurring on a regular basis and resulted in the bulk of calls to the Service Desk. Based on this information, he assembled teams to understand the problems that caused these incidents. The team's goal is to analyze these problems, determine the root cause, and once the error was known, eliminate it from the environment. If the error could not be eliminated, then the team was to document a workaround for that error and communicate the workaround to the Service Desk.

By realizing the value of Problem Management and approaching problems in a disciplined manner, Geppetto Garcia's IT organization moved from a reactive organization to a proactive organization. Through Problem Management, they established workarounds for commonly occurring incidents and managed their problems and errors through their lifecycle to resolution.

OVERVIEW

Problem Management is the process responsible for eliminating errors from the environment and reducing the incident volumes experienced by the users. Problem Management is also responsible for developing and publishing information that can assist in the rapid resolution of incidents. This information includes workarounds, publication of Known Errors, diagnostic scripts, and other information that can assist with the rapid resolution of incidents. This information becomes part of the Service Knowledge Management System (SKMS).

Purpose

The purpose of Problem Management is to prevent problems and the resulting incidents from occurring, as well as minimize the impact of incidents that cannot be prevented.

Problem Management performs the Root Cause Analysis (RCA) of problems to determine where the error is. Problem Management then converts this problem to a Known Error and manages the Known Error through resolution.

Problem Management also has a strong relationship with Knowledge Management and provides documented workarounds for the Service Knowledge Management System (SKMS). Problem Management should utilize the same tools as the other related processes, such as Incident Management.

Value to Business

Problem Management is where the reduction in Known Errors in the environment occurs resulting in improved availability and fewer incidents. Through this reduction in Known Errors, IT services have higher availability, users and IT staff increase productivity, and there is a reduction in the costs of firefighting or resolving repeat incidents.

Problem Management is also responsible for documenting workarounds to improve the resolution times of incidents. Proper Problem Management reduces the costs of these workarounds or fixes that do not work.

Key Concepts

Problem

A problem is defined as *the unknown cause of one or more incidents*. Problems, once diagnosed and the root cause is found, results in the documentation of a Known Error. A Known Error is defined as *a fault in the infrastructure for which a permanent solution or temporary workaround has been found*.

Problem Models

Similar to models that have been discussed elsewhere, Problem Models are established for the problems that are common to automate the documentation requirements and workflow.

Known Error Database

When the root cause of problems is determined, a Known Error is created and associated with its workaround or permanent fix. This information is stored in a Known Error database to be shared with the organization.

Tools and Techniques

Problem Management is a disciplined process that requires an analytical approach to determine the root cause of problems. Techniques are utilized by Problem Management to assist with the analysis of problems. These techniques include:

Chronological Analysis

Documenting the order of events that took place to determine how events relate to the problem.

Pain Value Analysis

Analyzing the broad view of the impact of the problem to determine the overall pain associated with the impact.

Kepner and Tregoe

Technique for formal problem investigation.

Brainstorming

Presenting ideas without regard to context and then applying the context.

Ishikawa Diagrams

Typically combined with brainstorming, Ishikawa Diagrams (also referred to as Fishbone Diagrams) analyze the cause and effect of events leading to a problem.

Pareto Analysis

Charting the symptoms of a problem to determine the main pain points.

These techniques are used to determine the overall pain associated with problems, as well as to identify the value associated with removing problems from the environment. Some problems, however, may be too complex, too costly, or not provide enough value for the pain associated to warrant the resources required to remove the underlying error. In these cases, workarounds are established to minimize the impact of the problem and underlying error.

ACTIVITIES

Problem Management is an undervalued process in many organizations. However, the activities in this process are important to manage problems and Known Errors through resolution.

Problem Detection

Detecting a problem could involve many tactics. Problem Management analyzes incident records for trends. These trends may identify potential problems. Single incidents may also result in opening a problem record to trigger further action.

Problem Logging

Problems are logged to ensure that all information regarding the problem is recorded. This information is updated over time as more information is determined regarding this problem.

Problem Categorization

Problems are categorized to determine which support group to route the problem to. Categorizations may be done by service, technology, application, or many other categorizations.

Problem Prioritization

Prioritization of problems is similar to that in Incident Management and Change Management. Prioritization is based on the urgency and impact. If the problem stemmed from an incident, the priority may already be determined. However, as the problem matures or more information is discovered about the problem, the priority may change.

Problem Investigation and Diagnosis

Problem investigation and diagnosis is where the root cause of the problem is determined. Once the root cause is determined, a Known Error is created and linked to its associated workarounds or permanent fixes.

Deploying Workarounds

Problem Management determines the appropriate workarounds for the problems. These workarounds are documented and recorded in the Known Error database so they can be shared with the rest of the organization. The Service Desk and Incident Management leverage these workarounds to resolve incidents as quickly as possible.

Raising a Known Error Record

Once the Known Error is determined, it is recorded and documented to ensure that it is managed through resolution.

Problem Resolution

When the problem is resolved, the resolution is tested and verified with the user to make sure that it resolves the problem and the error is removed.

Problem Closure

Similar to incidents, problems are formally closed to ensure that all associated documentation has been completed.

Major Problem Reviews

Some problems are large enough in scope that they may require reviews to determine and review both successes and failures. These reviews should be used as a way to improve the process.

Recording Errors from Development

Development and introduction of new services are a major source of introduction of problems into the environment. Any outstanding errors in newly released software or services should be recorded in Problem Management to ensure they are managed through resolution.

Monitoring and Tracking of Problems

Throughout the life of the problem, the problem is monitored and tracked through its lifecycle until it is resolved. This ensures that the problem obtains the appropriate attention that it needs.

Roles

A disciplined approach to Problem Management requires a Problem Manager to manage these problems and errors in the environment. The Problem Manager is responsible for ensuring that all of the activities in Problem Management are performed. However, the Problem Manager relies on the rest of the organization for these activities, including the root cause analysis, information development and determining solutions.

The specific responsibilities of the Problem Manager include:

> Communicate with all problem resolution groups
>
> Ownership and protection of the Known Error Database (KEDB)
>
> Formal closure of all Problem Records
>
> Develop and maintain relationships with suppliers and third parties with regard to solving problems
>
> Organizing and conducting major problem reviews

Problem groups, usually combinations of people from the Technical Management, Applications Management, and IT Operations Management functions, have the responsibility of resolving problems in the environment and removing the underlying error.

ACCESS MANAGEMENT

OVERVIEW

The Access Management process has overall responsibility for maintaining the security of services through ensuring that access is granted to only the people who require access for legitimate business reasons. Access Management does not decide who has access, but instead carries out the policies developed regarding access during the Service Design stage of the Service Lifecycle.

PURPOSE

The purpose of Access Management is to provide the rights for users to be able to use a service or group of services, as well as executing the policies and actions defined in Security Management and Availability Management. It is these other processes, which are determined in the Service Design stage of the Service Lifecycle, that determine what access should be provided and to whom it should be provided.

VALUE TO BUSINESS

Access Management assists with the overall security of the environment and its information. The value to business is that the business can be assured that its information is secure and access is provided to those who require the access. With proper Access Management, the business can be assured that access is controlled to confidential information, employees have the appropriate level of access, and that access can be audited if necessary. Business can also be assured that the organization is complying with regulatory requirements.

KEY CONCEPTS

Access is defined as *the level and extent of a service's functionality or data that a user is entitled to.*

Service Groups is defined as *the concept of establishing sets of services that users or groups of users are entitled to thus easing Access Management activities.* Service Groups identify users or services, or combinations of both, that are similar. Instead of providing access to a single individual for a single service, Service Groups are used so the user is added to the Service Group and thus is granted the rights as defined by the Service Group.

Identity is defined as *the information about them that distinguishes them as an individual and which verifies their status within the organization.* Identity will be established by one or more pieces of information such as an employee ID number, driver's license, passport, etc.

Directory Services is defined as *a specific type of tool that is used to manage access and rights.*

Rights is defined as *the actual setting whereby a user is provided access to a service or group of services.*

ACTIVITIES

The activities in Access Management involve not only managing access requests, but also responding to organizational, individual, or service changes that may impact access to information for a service.

Access Requests

When access is requested, Access Management processes the request. These requests can come from a number of sources for a number of reasons such as from Human Resources when an employee is hired, promoted, transferred or terminated. Requests for Change may also result in access being requested for a service. Service Requests that are processed by Request Fulfillment may also require access.

Verification

The verification activity involves determining who the user is and confirming they are who they say they are. This establishes the identity of the user. Based on the identity of the user, a determination is made that the user has a legitimate need to access the service.

Providing Rights

Access is provided to the user based on the policies and regulations defined in Service Strategy. Information Security Management also provide policies that define who has legitimate access to services.

Monitoring Identity Status

Access Management monitors the status of individuals. An individual's status may change due to promotions, demotions, transfers, termination, retirement, disciplinary action, or many other reasons. Based on changes in a user's status, the rights may require changing. Access Management adjusts the individual's rights based on such a change in status.

Logging and Tracking Access

Access to services is logged and tracked to ensure that an audit can be performed to determine who accesses which services. These logs may be required in the event of a security incident or other reason.

Removing or Restricting Rights

Access Management may require removing or restricting rights based on access abuse or changes in service. Information Security Management may also change policies which result in requiring removal or restriction of rights.

ROLES

There is no specific Access Manager. Instead, the activities within Access Management are performed by the Service Operation functions.

Service Desk

Requests for access go through the Service Desk as a regular Service Request. The Service Desk fulfills the requests that it is able to and escalates requests that the Service Desk cannot fulfill to the appropriate team for fulfillment.

Technical and Application Management

The Technical and Application Management functions may be responsible for the activities within Access Management. These functions fulfill the requests that the Service Desk is not able to fulfill. Technical and Access Management functions are also responsible for creating mechanisms to simplify and control Access Management, as well as testing the service to ensure access can be granted, controlled and prevented as designed.

IT Operations Management

The operational activities of Access Management may be delegated to IT Operations Management including verifying users and granting access.

CHAPTER REVIEW

Service Operation processes

> Incident Management
>
> Event Management
>
> Request Fulfillment
>
> Problem Management
>
> Access Management

Incident Management

Purpose

> Ensures that service is restored as quickly as possible and the adverse impact to the business is minimized.

Incident Models

> Pre-defined steps, responsibilities, timescales, escalation procedures and resolutions for commonly occurring incidents

Major Incidents

> Incidents with a high level of disruption to the business

Functional Escalation

> Forwarding an incident to a person or group with more specialized knowledge of that service or component

Hierarchical Escalation

> Forwarding an incident to a supervisor, manager, director, or further in order to notify them of the incident and possible impact, as well as to obtain resources to resolve an incident

Activities

Identification

Logging

Categorization

Prioritization

Initial Diagnosis

Investigation and Diagnosis

Resolution and Recovery

Closure

Roles

Incident Manager

Responsible for the overall process and ensuring that the activities in the process are carried out.

1st Level Support

Service Desk personnel responsible for the activities at the Service Desk when related to Incidents

2nd Level Support

Personnel with greater technical skill than the Service Desk

3rd Level Support

Internal teams and external vendors with specific knowledge required to resolve an Incident.

Event Management

Purpose

provides the ability to detect events, make sense of them and determine that the appropriate control action is provided

Event Types

Regular Operation

Exceptional

Unusual, but not Exceptional

Request Fulfillment

Purpose

Responsible for managing requests from users to ensure that they are addressed in a timely manner according to the organization's policies.

Problem Management

Purpose

To prevent problems and the resulting incidents from occurring as well as minimize the impact of incidents that cannot be prevented.

Problem

The unknown cause of one or more incidents.

Problem Models

Problem Models are established for the problems that are common to automate the documentation requirements and workflow.

Roles

Problem Manager

Responsible to ensure that all of the activities in Problem Management are performed.

Access Management

Purpose

To provide the rights for users to be able to use a service or group of services as well as executing the policies and actions defined in Security Management and Availability Management

Definitions

Access	The level and extent of a service's functionality or data that a user is entitled to
Service Groups	The concept of establishing sets of services that users or groups of users are entitled to thus easing Access Management activities
Identity	The information about them that distinguishes them as an individual and which verifies their status within the organization
Directory Services	A specific type of tool that is used to manage access and rights
Rights	The actual setting whereby a user is provided access to a service or group of services

Activities

Access Requests

Verification

Providing Rights

Monitoring Identity Status

Logging and Tracking Access

Removing or Restricting Rights

CHAPTER QUIZ

1. What are the processes described in Service Operation?

    a.   Information Security Management

    b.   Access Management

    c.   Problem Management

    d.   Event Management

    e.   Operations Management

    f.   Incident Management

    g.   Request Fulfillment

2. Incident Management has many purposes. What are three of them?

    a.   Remove problems and errors from the infrastructure

    b.   Ensure best use of resources

    c.   Restore normal operation as quickly as possible and minimize the impact of incidents

    d.   Ensure best possible levels of service

3. Incident models should include what?

    a.   Timescales

    b.   Escalation procedures

    c.   Chronological order of steps

    d.   Responsibilities

    e.   Workflow automation

4. Urgency and Impact determine what?

    a. Work order number

    b. Priority

    c. Escalation

    d. Resolution Timescales

5. The term used when an incident is forwarded to a specialized team is called what?

    a. Functional Referral

    b. Functional Escalation

    c. Hierarchic Escalation

    d. Workload Balancing

6. The term used when an incident is forwarded to someone with more authority is called what?

    a. Functional Referral

    b. Functional Escalation

    c. Hierarchic Escalation

    d. Workload Balancing

7. An event could trigger an Incident, Problem or Change.

    a. True

    b. False

8.   Match the role with its description:

    a.   Responsible for effectiveness and efficiency of the Incident Management process

    b.   Service Desk Personnel

    c.   Greater technical skill than the Service Desk

    d.   Internal technical groups or vendors

    i.   Third Line Support

    ii.   Second Line Support

    iii.   Incident Manager

    iv.   First Line Support

9.   The Event Manager is responsible for all the activities in Event Management.

    a.   True

    b.   False

10.   The process responsible for handling requests from the user is known as:

    a.   Change Management

    b.   Request Management

    c.   Incident Management

    d.   Request Fulfillment

11.   Which of the following is an example of a Service Requests?

    a.   A request to change the functionality of an application

    b.   A request for a new application to be developed

    c.   User requests the memory on their computer be upgraded

    d.   A request for a memory upgrade on a server

12. The process that is responsible to identify and remove errors from the infrastructure is what?

   a.   Problem Management

   b.   Error Control

   c.   Error Management

   d.   Incident Management

13. Problem Management has a strong relationship with which of the following processes?

   a.   Knowledge Management

   b.   Service Desk

   c.   Service Portfolio Management

   d.   Information Security Management

14. Increased availability of IT services is one benefit to business for Problem Management. The other values to business include what?

   a.   Reduced errors in newly released services

   b.   Reduced cost of workarounds

   c.   Higher productivity of business and IT staff

   d.   Reduction in reactive efforts

15. What are some of the techniques used in Problem Management?

   a.   Project Planning

   b.   Kepner and Tregoe

   c.   Pareto Analysis

   d.   Ishikawa Diagrams

   e.   Try and See

   f.   Brainstorming

16.   Access Management is also known as what? (pick 2)

    a.   Identity Management
    b.   Infrastructure Security Management
    c.   Security Management
    d.   Rights Management

17.   The term that refers to a specific type of tool that is used to manage access and rights is called what?

    a.   Identity
    b.   Directory Services
    c.   Access
    d.   Rights

18.   The term that refers to the actual settings whereby a user is provided access to service or group of services is called what?

    a.   Identity
    b.   Directory Services
    c.   Access
    d.   Rights

19.   The term that refers to the information about them that distinguishes them as an individual and which refers to their status within the organization is called what?

    a.   Identity
    b.   Directory Services
    c.   Access
    d.   Rights

20.   The term that refers to the level and extent of a service's functionality or data that a user is entitled to is called what?

a. Identify
b. Directory Services
c. Access
d. Rights

Answers

1. B, C, D, F, G
2. B, C, D
3. A, B, C, D
4. B
5. B
6. C
7. A
8. A – iii, B – iv, C – ii, D – i
9. B
10. D
11. C
12. A
13. A
14. B, C, D
15. B, C, D, F
16. A, D
17. B
18. D
19. A
20. C

15

CONTINUAL SERVICE IMPROVEMENT PROCESSES

OVERVIEW

One of the basic tenets of ITIL® is that we rarely do things perfectly the first time. Because of this, we should strive to build services and processes that have improvement mechanisms built in. Continual Service Improvement, provides guidance on how to build these improvements into our processes and services. If done correctly, Continual Service Improvement (CSI) is not a separate lifecycle stage, but is integrated into the other stages in the Service Lifecycle and their processes.

The only process in Continual Service Improvement is the 7-Step Improvement process.

Geppetto Garcia's

Mark Renner has noticed a disturbing trend in the IT department. Based on the recent history, Mark has noticed that the number of projects that succeed have declined over the past two years. Also, for those projects that do succeed, the result of the projects are almost obsolete when the project is completed.

Based on this trend, Mark did some research to find out why these projects were started in the first place. What Mark discovered is that the majority of improvements to IT services are based on some failure that occurred that required a redesign of the service or some major effort to improve the service. Mark also found that the business requirements evolved so quickly that the project to improve the service no longer met the requirements.

Mark looked for a solution to this predicament. What he discovered is that the improvement projects were often over-engineered to meet the actual need. Instead, what is needed is an approach to provide iterative, continual improvement for services that are targeted toward specific improvement activities. This focus on continual improvement would provide more targeted and smaller scale improvements over time as opposed to trying to improve everything at once. Mark turned to Continual Service Improvement for guidance.

7-Step Improvement Process

Overview

The 7-step improvement process is a formalized process to continually improve the quality of service to the customer. Improvements can be of many types, but commonly include reduction of costs, improved quality, and improving customer satisfaction. Quality of services is also a focus of the 7-step improvement process through improving the effectiveness and efficiency of IT Service Management as a discipline.

It is important to note that the 7-step improvement process is not necessarily focused on large-scale improvements. Small improvements should be considered as a regular way of doing business, as small-scale improvements can make a big difference over time.

Purpose

The purpose of the 7-Step Improvement process is to continually align and realign the service to the needs of the business. When a service is introduced, it is introduced to meet a specific business need. Over time, the needs of the business change and need to be re-evaluated. The 7-Step Improvement process ensures that the needs of the business are continually evaluated to re-align the service with the needs of the business.

Key Concepts

Knowledge Spiral

The 7-step Improvement process is supported by the Knowledge Spiral. The intent of the Knowledge Spiral is to improve organizational knowledge by collecting data, distilling information from it, obtaining knowledge from the information to facilitate making the right decisions, or providing wisdom. Data, Information, Knowledge and Wisdom are not synonymous.

The Knowledge Spiral is covered in more detail in the Knowledge Management process in the chapter on Service Transition.

Activities

The 7-step improvement process, shown in Figure 36, strives to improve all Service Lifecycle stages and spans the entire lifecycle. Nothing is out of scope for the process, including improvements in service, improvement in processes, improvements in quality and improvements in organization.

To begin the 7-step improvement process, it is important to first identify the vision and strategy of what needs to be improved. Based on this vision and strategy, tactical and operational goals are developed that support this strategy.

Step 1 – What Should You Measure?

The first step in the 7-step improvement process is to define what you should measure. Note the difference between what you should measure and what you can measure. If there is a difference between what you should measure and what you can measure, then there exists a gap that exposes an opportunity for improvement.

Many times, this determination of what should be measured will be determined in the Service Strategy and Service Design stages. However, even though it may have been determined in these stages doesn't mean that it is always the right determination. CSI strives to provide checks and balances with the other Service Lifecycle stages.

Step 2 – What Can You Measure?

Once it is documented what you should measure, it is time to determine what can be measured. This identification of what can be measured possibly determines service levels that can be measured, monitored and reported. This is determined through a gap analysis. Once it is determined what can be measured, it may provide a new service level that will be recorded in Service Level Agreements.

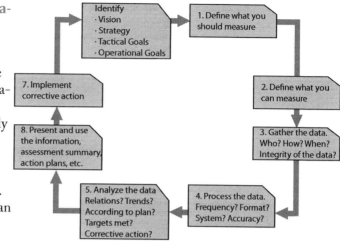

©Crown copyright 2007 - Reproduced under license from OGC

Figure 36 - Continual Service Improvement Process

The gap that results between what should be measured and what can be measured is an opportunity for improvement. It is highly likely that what can be measured is not the same as what should be measured. Improvements can be identified at this step to improve the service.

Step 3 – Gather Data

Data for continual improvement is gathered through the Service Operation stage of the Service Lifecycle. This is raw data that is collected and no conclusions are drawn from this data. This data may be both objective and subjective, and requires further analysis before drawing conclusions.

Step 4 – Process Data

Step four is to process the data and align the data with the Critical Success Factors (CSF's) and Key Performance Indicators (KPI's). The data should be bound by time frames such as per hour, per day, per week, etc. Gaps in the data become opportunities for improvement in the collection of the data. Data from multiple sources or data that is measured differently is normalized to obtain consistency.

Step 5 – Analyze Data

Step five is to analyze the data to develop information. Data analysis is often overlooked as people rush to draw conclusions from the raw data which may be useful, but is incomplete and may lead to wrong conclusions without proper perspective. Analysis of data to provide underlying trends reveals information that may not be revealed otherwise.

Step 6 – Present Information

The information developed from the data in step five is then presented. Presentation involves formatting the information so that it is more useful and communicative. This presentation presents an accurate picture of the results of the improvement efforts to help determine the next steps. Based on the data collected, analyzed and then presented, proper action can be taken to improve the service based on the overall vision, strategy and goals.

Step 7 – Implement Corrective Action

The seventh step is to implement corrective action based on the information developed from the collected data. In this step, permanent solutions are applied to the issues that have been discovered. Once implemented, the new state of the environment serves as a new baseline to establish continual improvement.

The corrective action identified may be identified through CSI, but other processes and other Service Lifecycle stages are responsible for implementing the corrective action.

Initiating a corrective action requires submitting an RFC to Change Management. This RFC is prioritized and categorized as any other. CSI works with Change Management as part of the CAB and takes an active role in Post Implementation Reviews (PIR's).

Release Management is responsible for moving the improvement into the production environment. As expected, the CSI improvement recommendations are enacted as any other suggested change to the environment.

Service Level Management conducts a Service Review with CSI to identify gaps in the service and suggest corrective action. These Service Reviews may involve the Availability Management and Problem Management processes.

ROLES

The roles in CSI include the Service Manager and the CSI Manager. The Service Manager role is one that encompasses the entire Service Lifecycle for a service while the CSI Manager is focused on the CSI stage of the Service Lifecycle for all services. Both roles (as with all other roles) are responsible for identifying opportunities of improvement.

Service Manager

The Service Manager is responsible for representing a specific service in its entirety. The Service Manager works with the Process Managers to ensure that the processes are in place to design, transition, operate and improve a service. The Service Manager works within these processes to represent the service where needed, such as in SLA review meetings and the Change Advisory Board. The Service Manager also works with the customers to ensure that the service is meeting the needs of the customer and identify opportunities for improvement.

The Service Manager is responsible for specific services and the following:

> Understanding the business strategy
>
> Assessing the competitive market
>
> Financial analysis of a service
>
> Managing vendors
>
> Delivery of management of the service utilizing the Service Lifecycle

CSI Manager

The CSI Manager is a new role within most IT organizations, but it is an important one. The CSI Manager has ultimate responsibility for the improvement activities to ensure that they are performed to ensure success regardless of the process or service. The CSI Manager works closely with Service Managers and Process Managers to improve the services and processes.

Chapter Review

7 Step Improvement Process

Purpose

Continually align and realign the service to the needs of the business

Activities

What should we measure

What can we measure

Gather data

Process data

Analyze data

Present data

Implement corrective action

Roles

Service Manager

Responsible for representing a specific service in its entirety

Continual Service Improvement Manager

Responsible for the improvement activities to ensure that they are performed to ensure success regardless of the process or service

CHAPTER QUIZ

1.   Continual Service Improvement is responsible for all metrics collection.

    a.   True
    b.   False

2.   In what activity does data become information?

    a.   Present and use the information
    b.   Process the data
    c.   Analyze the data
    d.   Normalize the data

3.   Put the steps in the 7-step improvement process in order.

    a.   Determine what you can measure
    b.   Gather the data
    c.   Determine what you should measure
    d.   Process the data
    e.   Present and use the information
    f.   Implement corrective action
    g.   Analyze the data

4. Which roles are responsible for identifying opportunities for improvement?

    a. Service Manager
    b. CSI Manager
    c. Process Manager
    d. All of the above

Answers

1. B
2. C
3. C, A, B, D, G, E, F
4. D

16

SERVICE OPERATION FUNCTIONS

OVERVIEW

Throughout this book, we have explored many processes with many activities in each one. The question that comes up often is "Who does all this work?" The answer is the functions described within Service Operation. Until now, organizational structures within IT have been largely left out. In this section the Service Operation functions are explored. It is these functions that perform a large number of the activities that we have discussed.

IT is supported by many organizations. These organizations are referred to as functions and have overall responsibility for ensuring the stability of the operational environment while responding to business needs. Remember that functions are defined as units of organizations specialized to perform certain types of work and responsible for specific outcomes. These functions include:

Service Desk

The Service Desk provides a single point of contact between users and IT Service Management. The Service Desk manages all calls from users including incidents, Service Requests, questions and feedback (praise and complaints).

Technical Management

Technical Management includes the technical teams responsible for the infrastructure that are usually organized by areas of expertise.

IT Operations Management

IT Operations Management is responsible for the ongoing day-to-day activities of IT. This function has two sub-functions of IT Operations Control and Facilities Management. IT Operations Control is responsible for the daily activities within IT including console management, job scheduling, backup, print and output, etc. Facilities Management is responsible for the physical environment of the data center and recovery sites.

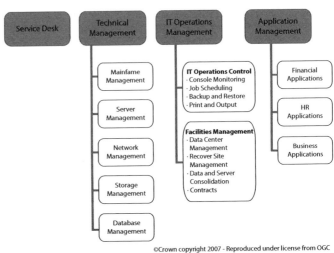

©Crown copyright 2007 - Reproduced under license from OGC

Figure 37 - Service Operation Functions

Application Management

Application Management involves the teams responsible for the specialty applications. Application Management is usually organized by area of specialty such as Financial Applications, Manufacturing Applications, etc.

The functions perform the activities in the processes from earlier chapters and rely on the processes for coordination across the functions.

SERVICE DESK

OVERVIEW

The Service Desk is the function that users of IT services interact with on a daily basis. From a user's perspective, this is the most critical function as the Service Desk is the only function the typical user interacts with directly. The Service Desk serves as the single point of contact between the Service Provider and the users. A typical Service Desk manages incidents and service requests, and also handles outward communication with the users.

Business finds a high performing Service Desk to be highly valued. The Service Desk provides this value through improving customer service, perception and satisfaction. A well-run, customer-oriented Service Desk can make up for a lot of imperfections within IT. How failures are handled can dramatically impact perception of value.

The Service Desk increases accessibility of users to IT. By providing a single point of contact for any user issue, question or request, IT becomes easier to work with from the user perspective. The Service Desk also improves communications with the users and business. By providing proactive status updates and informing users of additional services that may be of interest, the Service Desk becomes proactive in improving the productivity of the business. Through the Service Desk, it becomes apparent to the users and business that IT is there to help, instead of hinder.

Productivity of the users is only part of the benefit of a well-run Service Desk. The Service Desk also improves the productivity of IT by handling all calls that they can and escalating only the ones that they cannot. When escalated, the Service Desk coordinates the work of IT support resources by ensuring that the calls are escalated to the proper resources.

The Service Desk also provides IT with an understanding of the daily issues that users are experiencing. The Service Desk has the "pulse" of the users and understands the types of issues that they experience on a daily basis. This perspective can be communicated to IT to assist with identifying opportunities for improvement.

KEY CONCEPTS

SERVICE DESK STRUCTURES

There are many types of Service Desks. One of these is not necessarily better than the other. In fact, some organizations combined Service Desk structures and others provide multiple levels of Service Desks utilizing multiple structures.

Local Service Desk

The Local Service Desk is structured so that IT resources are co-located with the business. Wherever the business is, there is an IT organization in the same location. The local Service Desk only supports that local business unit.

This results in a greater ability to satisfy user requests but it can become very expensive as the IT resources are spread throughout the organization. This approach can also result in the IT resources in these disparate locations not using the same processes or tools.

Central Service Desk

The Central Service Desk is the opposite of the Local Service Desk. The Central Service Desk organizes all IT resources in one location regardless of the location of the business units. This results in a single point of contact for all users to contact IT.

With a Central Service Desk, all calls are routed to a single location. This results in providing less expensive support. However, this form of a Service Desk may not be able to provide support when local support resources are required. It may also leave users to feel isolated from support resources and the language or culture may be different between users and support – particularly for multi-national organizations.

Virtual Service Desk

The Virtual Service Desk is a Service Desk that utilizes technology to make it irrelevant where IT resources are located. With a Virtual Service Desk, IT resources can be located anywhere and still provide that central point of contact for their users.

With the proper tool support, the Virtual Service Desk ensures that the same processes are being used regardless of the location. A Virtual Service Desk can also optimize operational costs.

With a Virtual Service Desk, it is important to ensure that the tools used can support this Service Desk structure. The Virtual Service Desk may also result in not having the right staff in the right place when needed. A common language must be decided when recording information within organizations with different cultures and languages.

Follow the Sun

Many organizations use a "follow the sun" technique by transitioning call ownership to Service Desk facilities around the world based on times of day. For example, as the day ends in New York, the calls may be transitioned to Los Angeles for handling and resolution. When the day ends in Los Angeles, the calls may be transitioned to Asia. This transitioning continues based on time of day in an effort to support the business 24 hours per day.

SERVICE DESK CONSIDERATIONS

The Service Desk is a critical element in the delivery of consistent IT services. As such, there are many things to be considered. Each of these considerations is dependent on your unique IT environment.

Specialized Groups

Some services, particularly newly released services, required specialized knowledge. The Service Desk may opt to provide a specialized team to support these services. The specialized group may be staffed by other IT groups until the Service Desk has the knowledge to effectively support the service on their own.

Specialized groups are commonly used as part of Early Life Support when a large transition is taking place. Suppose that a new Time Management service is being transitioned and replacing the older Time Management system. Until the operations staff and the users have adjusted to the new service, a specialized group that focuses on this service may be established to ease the transition to the new service.

Building a Single Point of Contact

The Service Desk should be well publicized. Without knowledge of how to access the Service Desk, the users may not be able to benefit from the Service Desk. Adding the Service Desk phone number, web site and other contact points to a web portal, stickers on the phone, and organizational news letters are only a few ways to publicize the Service Desk.

Staffing

Demand for the Service Desk may be highly volatile. There may be certain times of the day, week, month or year where demand is greater than others. To determine when this demand occurs, the call rates should be analyzed to determine when demand is highest. To satisfy demand the Service Desk should consider part-time workers, home workers, or virtual workers.

Service Desk Training

The Service Desk requires a unique combination of skills and abilities in order to be most effective. Not only does the Service Desk require technical expertise to resolve incidents, but more importantly, requires customer service skills to be able to communicate effectively with the users.

The Service Desk should also have knowledge of the business. This knowledge helps the Service Desk communicate better with the users by being able to communicate with them on their terms. The Service Desk should understand what the users are tasked with accomplishing so they can support these tasks more effectively.

Training at the Service Desk can involve mentoring or shadowing. A person working on the Service Desk may be mentored by someone more senior to pass along the knowledge they have obtained. Shadowing is another technique where Service Desk staff shadow other organizations to understand better what activities are involved within IT that the Service Desk supports.

Staff Retention

Losing Service Desk staff can be very costly and disruptive to the effectiveness of the Service Desk. It is important to understand the value of the Service Desk and the im-

Service Desk Staffing

Many years ago, a popular microprocessor manufacturer that I worked for was found to have a flaw in the floating point arithmetic in one of their chips.

They satisfied their customers by offering to replace these chips with fault-free chips free of charge. As expected, the call volumes from customers rose substantially.

The company supplemented their Service Desk by rotating non-Service Desk employees onto the phones to meet this increased volume.

portance of the people who staff the Service Desk. The Service Desk is often a stepping stone to other roles, and staff retention can be improved by preparing the individuals for this new role. Even though an individual may leave the Service Desk to assume a new role in the organization, it serves as a greater motivator to others than if they were to leave the company.

Super Users

In some organizations, there are users who may be leveraged to provide support above and beyond what the Service Desk provides. These super users may have knowledge of specific applications, business functions, or business processes. These super users may be utilized to train Service Desk staff and can also be considered to be an extension of the Service Desk.

These super users can be a conduit for communications both into the Service Desk and from the Service Desk. As such, incident "storms" can be avoided by streamlining communications when a failure occurs. However, an incident, regardless of how it is communicated to the Service Desk, must still be logged.

The Service Desk can be a high-stress and often thankless job. The environment that the Service Desk staff operates in should be conducive to lowering these stresses as much as possible. Providing an area that is well-lit, quiet, with adequate space and break areas can play a large role in Service Desk staff satisfaction.

Service Desk Staffing Considerations

Staffing the Service Desk can be problematic. There are times when there may be too many people and times when there may not be enough. To better staff the Service Desk, the following factors should be considered:

Customer Service Expectations

Response times are an important consideration in staffing levels. If there is a high requirement for responsiveness, staffing levels will be higher.

Business Requirements

The most important consideration for staffing is the business requirements. What business expects from the Service Desk will impact the staffing levels. If business is largely self-supporting, the staffing levels will be lower.

Customers and Users

The customers and users are an important consideration. Customers and users that are diverse have diverse support requirements. Language, culture, skill levels and abilities for self-support affect support level requirements at the Service Desk.

Service Desk Abilities

The abilities of the Service Desk staff should be considered. Service Desks with a high level of ability may not require high staffing levels. However, Service Desk staff with a low level of ability and who only serve as a pass-through for calls may require lower staffing levels. A balance between ability and staffing levels must be achieved.

Processes and procedures can assist with lowering staffing levels. If well-defined processes and procedures are in place, they can be followed routinely to increase responsiveness to calls.

Support Aspects

Considerations should be given for what type of support is required; telephone, email, in person, remote control, and video are only a few considerations. Different levels of support access have different staffing levels. In person support, for example requires someone to be in a particular place at a particular time. In contrast, remote control technologies remove this requirement.

Training can also be an important aspect – both for the support staff, as well as the users. Highly trained users do not require as high level of support. Additionally, constant turnover at the Service Desk requires a higher level of training for the Service Desk staff.

In any case, technology considerations should be made to determine how best to utilize technology to lessen staffing requirements. The proper use of technology can minimize staffing requirements.

ACTIVITIES

The Service Desk's main activity is to manage calls that come in. When we refer to calls, we refer to any form of contact with the Service Desk. These calls could be in the form of a telephone call, email, walk up, pager, web submission or even fax. Your organization will determine the accepted forms of contact to the Service Desk.

Managing Calls

When a call comes in, the Service Desk ensures that it is logged and all relevant details are recorded. Based on the call, the Service Desk will allocate the proper categorization and prioritization. These calls can be one of four basic types. These types include:

Incidents

The user has been interrupted by some failure, or perceived failure, in the IT environment

Service Requests

The user requests access to some service defined in the Service Catalog

Questions/Information

The user requires some information regarding an outstanding call or regarding some service

Feedback

The user wants to provide feedback, both positive (compliments) and negative (complaints) regarding service

Managing Incidents and Service Requests

When responding to an Incident or Service Request, the Service Desk performs the following activities:

Provides first-line investigation and diagnosis

The Service Desk provides the initial investigation and diagnosis of an incident to determine where the true nature of that incident is.

Resolving incidents and Service Requests

The Service Desk resolves incidents and Service Requests which they can. Over time, the ability of the Service Desk will increase to resolve more and more incidents and Service Requests as their knowledge improves. The key to being able to resolve incidents and Service Requests is ensuring that the Technical Management and Application Management functions take the time to relay information on how to resolve incidents and Service Requests to the Service Desk.

Escalating incidents and service requests that cannot be resolved within agreed time scales

Many incidents and Service Requests cannot be resolved by the Service Desk. While it is preferred that the Service Desk have the ability to resolve all incidents and Service Requests, it is highly unlikely that this will ever happen as some of these incidents and Service Requests require detailed knowledge.

When the Service Desk cannot resolve an incident or Service Request, the Service Desk will escalate it to be resolved by someone with more technical expertise

Closing all resolved incident, requests and other calls

The Service Desk has the responsibility of ensuring that incidents and Service Requests are closed and the resolution meets the needs of the submitter.

This provides the ability to provide feedback to the user to ensure that the incident and Service Request are properly managed.

This activity ensures that no calls to the Service Desk are lost, forgotten, or ignored.

Communications

Communication with users is more than just waiting for a call to come in. The Service Desk also provides out-bound communication regarding interruptions to service, new services, or changed services. Examples of communications from the Service Desk include: informing users of progress of their calls; and conducting customer and user satisfaction call backs and surveys

Updating the CMS

When the Service Desk receives a call, the Service Desk verifies that the information contained in the CMS represents what the user sees. These "mini-audits" are checking basic information to ensure that the CMS reflects the actual environment.

Key Performance Indicators

Service Desk Key Performance Indicators (KPI's), or metrics, are focused on calls to the Service Desk. These metrics are used to evaluate the health, maturity, efficiency and effectiveness of the Service Desk, as well as to determine staffing requirements and areas of improvement.

These Key Performance Indicators (KPI's) include:

First-line resolution rates

Refers to the resolutions provided by the Service Desk without relying on other staff.

First call resolution

The resolutions provided almost immediately upon the first call to the Service Desk.

Average time to resolve

This metric shows the average resolution time from initiation of the call to closure.

Average time to escalate

This metric shows the average time each call stays at the Service Desk before it is escalated to other support staff.

Average cost of handling

The average cost of calls, incidents, questions and feedback should be determined and recorded by type of call.

This can be calculated a number of ways, such as the total cost of the Service Desk divided by the number of calls to the Service Desk. This calculates the cost per call. Another way to calculate this metric is to take the total cost of the Service Desk divided by the total time the calls are in progress. This calculates the cost per minute or other time unit.

Average time to review and close a call

Once a call is resolved, it should be reviewed and formally closed. This metric shows the average time it takes for a review and formal closure.

Calls by time of day, week, etc.

Determining call volumes by day, time of day, week, etc., provides information regarding call patterns and when additional staffing may be required.

CRITICAL SUCCESS FACTORS

The Service Desk is critical in supporting the Incident Management process. Because of this, the Service Desk and Incident Management should follow the same process. In many organizations, but not all, the Service Desk is responsible for the entire Incident Management process, so the two are very closely related.

To be most effective, the Service Desk must have access to information and people who understand the services being supported. Much of the information, such as incident record history, is the responsibility of the Service Desk. However, other information is provided to the Service Desk from outside the Service Desk. Problem records, Known Errors, the Change Schedule, alerts from monitoring tools, and the Service Knowledge Management System (SKMS) are some of the information provided to the Service Desk from IT.

The Service Desk should also have access to the Configuration Management System (CMS). When responding to incidents, the Service Desk uses the CMS to better understand the nature of the incident and also updates the CMS when necessary should any configuration errors be discovered.

Service Level Agreements are also provided to the Service Desk to ensure that the Service Desk understands the levels of service that have been agreed to. Without the SLAs, the Service Desk cannot prioritize incidents. This is particularly true when incidents occur for services that have variable priorities. An example of this type of service is Financial Reporting. Financial Reporting is typically most important at the end of the quarter, and particularly at the end of the year, when financial reports must be completed within a specific time period to meet regulatory requirements.

The Service Desk should publish response times and possibly resolution times for calls made to the Service Desk. However, the Service Desk is not solely responsible for the services that the users call about. The rest of IT is readily involved in providing ongoing support of these services.

In order for the Service Desk to accurately publish response and resolution times, the Service Desk must be supported by agreements and contracts from the rest of the organization. Operational Level Agreements (OLA's) are agreements between IT organizations that specify how the organizations support each other, as well as expectations for that support. OLA's are critical between the Service Desk and the organizations that provide support for the Service Desk.

Services are also supported by external vendors through contracts. These contracts should be communicated to the Service Desk to enable the Service Desk to publish reaction and response times accordingly.

As can be realized from the above sources of information and support for the Service Desk, an effective Service Desk is not the responsibility of the Service Desk alone. The Service Desk must be supported by all parts of IT in order to be most effective and efficient.

TECHNICAL MANAGEMENT

OVERVIEW

Technical Management is the function responsible for providing technical skills in support of IT services and management of the IT infrastructure. The Technical Management Function involves the various teams required in order to design, deliver, support and continually improve IT services. These teams are typically organized by specialty, such as the database team, the server administration team, the desktop support team and others.

OBJECTIVES

The objective of the Technical Management function is to help plan, implement and maintain a stable technical infrastructure through designing a highly resilient, cost effective and technical topology, the use of adequate technical skills to maintain the technical infrastructure in optimum condition, and the swift use of technical skills to diagnose and resolve technical failures that occur. The Technical Management function has responsibilities through the entire Service Lifecycle, not just Service Operation.

DUAL ROLE

Technical Management has a dual role within IT. While Technical Management provides stability to an organization, Technical Management must also be responsive to the business needs. The Technical Management Function's responsibilities are to provide resources to support services through the Service Lifecycle. In addition, the teams are called upon to provide knowledge and information regarding the services and the components that make up the services.

The Technical Management Function is called upon in every process to perform the numerous activities in these processes. The activities involve every aspect of the Service Lifecycle to develop strategy (particularly providing input to the Service Portfolio and Service Catalog), design the service, transition the service into operation, support the service through its operation, and continually improve the service over time.

Organizational Considerations

Within the Technical Management Function, considerations must be made in order to best optimize staffing levels. In an ideal world, the most specialized resources would be hired to provide support for our services. However, these specialized resources can be very expensive, so a balance must be achieved between the specialization and skill levels of resources, as well as the costs associated with those resources.

As a result, Technical Management staffing is often taken from pools of technical resources. In particular, teams of specialists are assembled for project related work and also to resolve problems.

Highly specialized work may involve the use of contractors or specialized external staff. While external staff can be quite expensive, it is likely that the work can be done quicker through the knowledge and specialized skills of such staff.

APPLICATION MANAGEMENT

OVERVIEW

The Application Management function is the function responsible for managing applications through their lifecycle. This responsibility includes applications within the infrastructure, regardless of whether they are developed in house or externally procured. Most of the time, this includes the core application sets that are critical to business processing, or highly specialized, such as the ERP system or other highly specialized, complex applications.

OBJECTIVES

Application Management works with Technical Management to identify functional and manageability requirements for application software to support the business processes, assist in the design and deployment of applications, and assist in the ongoing support and improvement of applications.

To accomplish these objectives, the applications must be well designed, resilient and cost effective. Through application rollout, the required functionality must be available to achieve the required business outcome. Also, Application Management must ensure it maintains adequate technical skills to operate applications in optimum condition, and to swiftly diagnose and resolve any technical failures.

The major decision that must be made with application support is whether to build versus buy an application. Different organizations will approach this decision differently based on strategy, culture, capabilities and other considerations.

A common misconception is that an application is a service. While an application may play a critical role in providing a service, the service involves far more than an application. It also includes the people, processes, underlying technology, and partners required to deliver and support the business desired outcomes provided, in part, by the application.

Dual Role

Application Management has a dual role within IT. While Application Management provides stability to an organization, Application Management must also be responsive to the business needs. The Application Management function's responsibilities are to provide resources to support services through the Service Lifecycle. In addition, the teams are called upon to provide knowledge and information regarding the services and the components that make up the services.

The Application Management function is called upon in every process to perform the numerous activities in these processes. The activities involve every aspect of the Service Lifecycle to develop strategy (particularly providing input to the Service Portfolio and Service Catalog), design the service, transition the service into operation, support the service through its operation, and continually improve the service over time.

Organizational Considerations

Application Management guides IT Operations in how best to manage applications in the Service Operation stage of the Service Lifecycle, but also designs management of the applications in the Service Design stage. Therefore, Application Management should be integrated into the entire IT Service Management lifecycle to ensure that the application lifecycle is understood and is integrated into specific points in the Service Lifecycle.

Note that Application Management is a separate responsibility from Application Development. Application Management assists Application Development in determining the requirements, application design, application testing, rollout and operation of the application. Application Development has the responsibility of developing the application.

IT Operations Management

Overview

The IT Operations Management is the function within an IT Service Provider which performs the daily activities needed to manage IT Services and the supporting IT infrastructure. IT Operations management accomplishes this by maintaining the status quo to achieve stability of the organization's day-to-day activities and processes. This requires regular scrutiny and improvements to achieve improved service at reduced cost.

IT Operations Management must also utilize swift application of operational skills to diagnose and resolve any IT operations failures that may occur. Driven by procedures, IT Operations Management records this knowledge to provide operational workflow that improves the speed of resolution.

IT Operations Management, just like Technical Management and Applications Management, has a dual role. However, IT Operations Management must balance the requirement for infrastructure stability with the requirement to change according to business needs.

To achieve balance between these roles it requires an understanding of how technology is used to provide IT service as well as understanding of the relative impacts of services on business. The value of IT Operations Management should be based on Return on Investment (ROI), not cost. By communicating the ROI of the function, the value of the IT Operations Management can more easily be discerned.

Characteristics

The IT Operations Management function differs from the Technical Management and Application Management functions in that it focuses on operational activities directly in line with specific business processes, such as manufacturing or product distribution. The

IT Operations Management Function provides specific activities that are well defined and repeatable to support these business activities. These activities include ensuring that a device, system or process is running or working as expected.

IT Operations Management focuses on shorter-term activities and improving those activities, not projects. Using specialized technical staff, IT Operations Management performs these daily activities to build repeatable, consistent action to ensure success.

This function is where the value of the organization is delivered and measured. To provide this value, IT Operations Management requires an investment in equipment, people, or both.

OPERATIONS CONTROL AND FACILITIES MANAGEMENT

The IT Operations Management Function includes two sub-functions; Operations Control and Facilities Management. Operations Control is also known as the Network Operation Center (NOC), Operations Bridge, and many other names. Operations Control is primarily responsible for ensuring that business processes are running to support the business. This is usually accomplished through monitoring via Event Management.

Operations Control's responsibilities include performing specific tasks, such as console management, job scheduling, backup and restore, print and output management, as well as maintenance activities. These responsibilities are activity-based as opposed to project-based. Operations Control focuses exclusively on individual activities and improving these activities. Project-based activities are the responsibility of other functions.

The Facilities Management aspect of IT Operations Management is responsible for maintenance of the physical environment. Specific examples include the data center, recovery sites, power and other environmental controls such as Heating, Ventilation and Air Conditioning (HVAC).

Facilities Management, unlike Operations Control, is involved in some project-based activities. Typical project-based activities that Facilities Management would be involved with include server consolidation efforts and data center consolidation efforts. Projects related to recovery sites would also involve Facilities Management

ORGANIZATIONAL OVERLAP

While it is easy to visualize Application Management, Technical Management and IT Operations Management as separate functions, often they are not. These functions may not be clearly delineated from one function to another. Therefore, an organizational overlap occurs where these lines of demarcation are not clear. An organization may combine the responsibilities of these functions into a single organization.

Chapter Review

Service Operations Functions

Service Desk

Technical Management

IT Operations Management

Applications Management

Service Desk

Purpose

Single point of contact between the Service Provider and the users

Service Desk Structures

Local Service Desk

Central Service Desk

Virtual Service Desk

Follow-The-Sun

Service Desk Considerations

Specialized Groups

Building a Single Point of Contact

Staffing

Service Desk Training

Staff Retention

Super Users

Activities

Managing Calls

Managing Incidents and Service Requests

Provides first-line investigation and diagnosis

Resolving incidents and Service Requests

Escalating incidents and service requests

Closing all resolved incident, requests and other calls

Technical Management

Purpose

Responsible for providing technical skills in support of IT services and management of the IT infrastructure.

Dual Role

Provide resources to support services through the Service Lifecycle

Provide knowledge and information regarding the services and the components that make up the service

Application Management

Purpose

Responsible for managing applications through their lifecycle

Dual Role

Provide resources to support services through the Service Lifecycle

Provide knowledge and information regarding the services and the components that make up the service

IT Operations Management

Purpose

Performs the daily activities needed to manage IT Services and the supporting IT infrastructure

Sub-Functions

Operations Control

Responsible for ensuring that business processes are running to support the business

Facilities Management

Responsible for maintenance of the physical environment.

Organizational Overlap Between

Technical Management

Application Management

IT Operations Management

CHAPTER QUIZ

1.   Service Operations Functions include what?

   a.   Service Desk

   b.   Vendor Management

   c.   Applications Management

   d.   IT Operations Management

   e.   Technical Management

   f.   Software Engineering

2.   The Applications Management function includes the teams that are responsible for applications development.

   a.   True

   b.   False

3.   The function that is responsible to be the single point of contact between the Service Provider and the users is called what?

   a.   IT Operations Management

   b.   Service Desk

   c.   Technical Management

   d.   Applications Management

4.   The function that is responsible for managing incidents and calls is called what?

   a.   IT Operations Management

   b.   Service Desk

   c.   Technical Management

   d.   Applications Management

5.   Match the Service Desk structure with the description:

   a.   Support staff is co-located with the business
   b.   Support staff is located in one place
   c.   Support staff is located anywhere in the world
   d.   Calls are transitioned between groups depending on the time of day

   i.   Virtual Service Desk
   ii.   Local Service Desk
   iii. Follow the Sun
   iv.   Central Service Desk

6.   What is the term used for users with exceptional knowledge of a service that may assist the Service Desk with service-related issues?

   a.   Trained Users
   b.   Super Users
   c.   Special Users
   d.   Application Developers

7.   What are two things that must be considered prior to the Service Desk committing to a specific level of service?

   a.   Underpinning contracts
   b.   Service Level Agreements (SLA's)
   c.   Operational Level Agreements (OLA's)
   d.   Operational Schedules

8. What things must the Service Desk have access to in order to be most efficient and effective?

  a. All incident records
  b. Problem Records
  c. Known Errors
  d. Change Schedule
  e. SKMS
  f. CMS
  g. All of the above

9. The function that is responsible for providing technical skills in support of IT Services and management of the IT infrastructure is called what?

  a. Service Desk
  b. Applications Management
  c. Technical Management
  d. IT Operations Management

10. The function that is responsible for managing Applications throughout their Lifecycle is called what?

  a. Applications Management
  b. Technical Management
  c. IT Operations Management
  d. Service Desk

11. Technical Management has a dual role. What are these two roles?

  a. Maintain application knowledge to be highly effective
  b. Ensure the single point of contact with the users
  c. Be custodians of technical information with regard to the infrastructure
  d. Provide resources to support the Service Lifecycle

12.   The function that is responsible for performing the daily activities needed to manage IT services and the supporting IT infrastructure is called what?

    a.   Technical Management

    b.   IT Operations Management

    c.   Service Desk

    d.   Applications Management

13.   IT Operations Control is also known as what (pick 2)?

    a.   Infrastructure Management

    b.   Job Scheduling

    c.   Network Operations Center

    d.   Operations Bridge

14.   IT Operations Management includes what other two functions?

    a.   Job Scheduling

    b.   Operations Control

    c.   Facilities Management

    d.   Infrastructure Management

Answers

1.   A, C, D, E
2.   B
3.   B
4.   B
5.   A – ii, B – iv, C – i, D – iii
6.   B
7.   B, C
8.   G
9.   C
10. A
11. C, D
12. B
13. C, D
14. B, C

17

TOOL AND TECHNOLOGY CONSIDERATIONS

OVERVIEW

Throughout this book, we have focused on processes. Processes, however, require the effective use of technology to support them and provide automation of the workflow within the process. In this chapter, some of the tools and technology considerations to support these processes are explored.

While ITIL promotes a structured, disciplined, and process oriented approach IT Service Management, it is apparent that this cannot be accomplished without the use of tools and technology to assist. However, tools cannot implement these processes for an organization. The tools are only as good as the process that they support.

Technology exists that assist greatly in automating good processes. This technology also assists in automating bad processes. The important consideration here is to ensure that the technology supports the processes, not defines the processes.

There are many reasons for turning to technology to assist with processes. People have a limited capacity for dealing with the inherent complexities of socio-technical systems. IT Service Management and its services are socio-technical systems. We cannot process as much information as a tool can to distill the information into what is truly important. Additionally, tools can assist with determining how the sub-systems affect each other.

SERVICE AUTOMATION

Service automation applies technology to automate routine activities and procedures. Through the use of service automation, the utility and warranty of services are improved. Service automation also assists with critical decision making during design and operation of services, including automating and documenting workflow, adjusting capacity, balancing workload, and optimizing the scheduling, routing and allocation of services and the resources they consume. Service automation also helps to document the activities in a service, as well as capture knowledge of a service.

Many of the concepts that have been explored in this book are candidates for service automation. Some of these include:

> Design and modeling of services
>
> The Service Catalog
>
> Pattern recognition and analysis (such as trend analysis)
>
> Classification, prioritization and routing of incidents, problems, Service Requests and changes
>
> Detection and monitoring
>
> Service optimization

Think about how banking, getting gas for your car, or travel has changed over the last two decades. All of these industries are now assisted by service automation technology such as ATM machines, self-serve pumping machines and airline check-in kiosks that provide us the instant service that we have come to expect.

SERVICE STRATEGY TOOLS

Part of Service Strategy is to understand how tools and technology can assist as a compensating factor for deficiencies in a service. Tools and technology can compensate for poor design, poor processes and inadequate knowledge. While Service Strategy should work to improve design, processes and knowledge, it cannot be done without the use of technology.

Service Strategy benefits from simulation tools to evaluate the consequences of decisions prior to implementing them. Analytical models are used to evaluate the allocation of resources, as well as analyze demand patterns. Other tools used by Service Strategy include decision trees, queuing and work flow models, forecasting models and analyzing variance of demand and resources.

SERVICE DESIGN TOOLS

Service Design tools involve the use of tools to enable better design. These tools can speed up design, provide a higher quality design, provide analysis of design options, as well as ensure that the design meets the requirements of the business. Tools used in Service Design can also ensure that standards and conventions are followed.

Modeling and prototyping are common types of tools used in Service Design to assist with optimizing the design of services and conducting "what if" analysis. These tools also ensure that interfaces and dependencies have been considered and validate the design of services to ensure they meet business requirements.

Some of the areas that design tools assist with include:

> Hardware and software design
> Environmental design
> Process design
> Data design

SERVICE TRANSITION TOOLS

Service Transition tools can be classified into two types. Enterprise tools include the tools that address the larger issue of IT Service Management. These tools are usually well integrated to provide a holistic approach to IT Service Management. At the core of many of these tools is the Configuration Management Database that implements the CMS. Also, these tools usually include many types of support for network management, topology mapping, incident handling, service requests, change management and many other areas.

Targeted Service Transition tools can be of many types to support the various activities of Service Transition. These tools are not limited to Service Transition activities, but may also provide support for other stages as well.

Specifically, these tools include the following types:

Knowledge Management tools

Knowledge Management tools retain and propagate organizational knowledge. These tools assist with the management of documents, records and content.

Collaboration tools

Collaboration tools provide focused support for groups or teams that provide facilities for communication. Examples of collaboration tools include shared calendars, instant messaging and email.

Workflow Management

Workflow management tools assist with the automation of workflow, procedures or processes, as well as assist with workflow design, object routing and event services.

Configuration Management System (CMS)

The CMS contains details about the attributes and history of each CI and details important relationship between CI's.

The Definitive Media Library (DML) may be included.

SERVICE OPERATION TOOLS

The Service Operation stage of the Service Lifecycle is where the value is delivered to the business. The processes in this stage involve communication, organization and reporting. Tools and technology are required within this stage to facilitate this communication, organization and reporting. Since the processes in this stage, Incident Management, Problem Management, Request Fulfillment and Event Management are so closely inter-twined, it is expected that the tools for this stage of the Service Lifecycle support these processes in an integrated manner. These tools should also include integration to Service Asset and Configuration Management's CMS, Change Management and Service Level Management.

The use of tools should also promote user self-help. A self-help solution available to the users provides knowledge of the services and assists with communication between IT and the users. This can reduce the staffing requirements at the Service Desk to provide support. The Service Desk can also benefit from tools through the use of an integrated approach to requests, problems, incidents, and any models or pre-defined workflow that can be developed within these tools. These tools can also provide direct access to the back-end automated processes such as downloading new software to the desktop.

Discovery tools also can be leveraged to automate many of the activities involved in ensuring the environment is well-controlled and unauthorized changes are detected. These tools can also support the Service Operation stage of the Service Lifecycle through software distribution and license management.

Other tools can be leveraged to provide remote control facilities that provide the ability to take over a user's computer remotely. Other diagnostic utilities should be considered as appropriate to better understand and resolve errors.

Reporting is a critical component of Service Operation to report how IT is meeting the needs of the business. Reporting tools should be considered to improve and automate reporting requirements. Part of the reporting may be provided through dashboards that show at a glance the overall operation of IT. As the IT organization matures and report-ing is improved, integration to the business will show how technology relates to the busi-ness and how IT supports the business desired outcomes. This is called Business Service Management.

Chapter Review

Service automation

Applies technology to automate routine activities and procedures.

Service Design Tools

Assists with

Hardware and software design

Environmental design

Process design

Data design

Service Transition Tools

Types

Knowledge Management tools

Collaboration tools

Workflow Management

Configuration Management System (CMS)

Service Operation Tools

Self-help tools

Discovery tools

Reporting

Dashboards

Diagnostic utilities

CHAPTER QUIZ

1.   With the right technology or tool solution, you don't need to worry about process.

   a.   True
   b.   False

2.   What area can benefit from Service Automation?

   a.   Design and modeling
   b.   Pattern recognition and analysis
   c.   Detection and monitoring
   d.   Optimization
   e.   All of the above

3.   Match the Service Operation tool type with its description:

   a.   Automates and verifies the CMS
   b.   Provides ability to take control of a user's desktop
   c.   Assists with diagnostic activities
   d.   Allows easy viewing of information
   e.   Provides high-level visibility of IT service performance
   f.   Relates technology to business

   i.   Reporting
   ii.   Dashboards
   iii.   Remote Control
   iv.   Discovery/Deployment/Licensing tools
   v.   Business Service Management
   vi.   Diagnostic Utilities

4. Design tools assist with which of the following types of design?

    a. Hardware design
    b. Software design
    c. Environmental design
    d. Process design
    e. Data design
    f. All of the above

Answers

1. B
2. E
3. A – iv, B – iii, C – vi, D – i, E – ii, F – v
4. F

Index